DON'T GET STUCK ON STUPID!

DON'T GET STUCK ON STUPID!

Leadership In Action

LT. GENERAL
RUSSEL L. HONORÉ

(U.S. Army, Retired)

With Mark B. Robson
& Leigh Hennessy Robson

Acadian House
PUBLISHING
Lafayette, Louisiana

ON THE COVER: *Lt. General Russel Honoré directs the search-and-rescue effort in New Orleans, La., in September 2005 following Hurricane Katrina. A tough-talking, take-charge Army general at the time, Honoré has since retired and, by the way, has given up the cigars. His new role: public speaker, business consultant and advisor on matters related to disaster preparedness and recovery, (Carlos Barria / Reuters)*

Library of Congress Cataloging-in-Publication Data

Names: Honore, Russel L., author. | Robson, Mark B., author. | Robson, Leigh Hennessy, author.
Title: Don't get stuck on stupid! : leadership in action / LT. General Russel L. Honore (U.S. Army, Retired) ; with Mark B. Robson & Leigh Hennessy Robson.
Description: Lafayette, LA : Acadian House Publishing, [2018] | Includes bibliographical references and index.
Identifiers: LCCN 2017055682| ISBN 9780999588413 (pbk. : alk. paper) | ISBN 0999588419 (pbk. : alk. paper)
Subjects: LCSH: Social problems--United States. | Leadership--United States. | United States--Social conditions--21st century. | United States--Politics and government--21st century.
Classification: LCC HN59.2 .H6325 2018 | DDC 306.0973--dc23 LC record available at https://lccn.loc.gov/2017055682

♦ Published by Acadian House Publishing, Lafayette, Louisiana
  (Edited by Trent Angers; editorial assistance and research by Darlene Smith; interior pre-press production by Leah Ewing)
♦ Cover design and production by Glenn Noya, New Orleans, Louisiana
♦ Printed by Royal Palm Press, Punta Gorda, Florida

To the ones I love:
Family, Friends, America
and my horse, Big Red

Acknowledgements

I am eternally grateful to the many people who worked with me to make this book a reality.

First and foremost, I must thank my wife, Beverly Honoré, who always believes I am capable of great things and without whom I would not be the man I am today; my daughter and scheduler, Stefanie Honoré Acosta; and my daughter Kimberly Honoré, my social media advisor who helps me keep up to date on local and world affairs.

Thanks especially to Mark B. Robson and Leigh Hennessy Robson, my co-writers who were with me every step of the way. They spent countless hours with me discussing the topics in this book, followed by impeccable research and writing to bring these important ideas to life.

In addition, this book would not have been possible without editor Trent Angers and his colleague Darlene Smith at Acadian House Publishing.

Other key people who provided invaluable guidance and suggestions were Cynthia Belton of the U.S. Department of Homeland Security, Professor Oliver A. Houck of Tulane University Law School, Green Army operations officer Jacques Morial, and Camille L. Stauber of Sustainable Places, Inc.

Several people read various chapter galleys to help assure accuracy. These include Drew Hoffmann of the Louisiana Tax Commission and Bob Anderson, an environmental journalist who spent many years reporting for *The* (Baton Rouge) *Advocate*. Also helping with fact-checking were three devoted defenders of the environment: Bill Goodell, Kim Goodell and Vic Hummert, all of Lafayette, La.

I would also like to thank my two sons for continuing the family tradition of military service going back to the Revolutionary War: Sergeant First Class Michael Honoré, Sapper Platoon Sergeant, and First Lieutenant Steven Honoré, Infantry Platoon Leader.

Finally, I must acknwledge my horse, Big Red, who keeps me sane and who constantly reminds me that there is an alternative to being stuck on stupid.

Approaching old problems with fresh eyes

I will never forget the first time I met Lt. Gen. Russel Honoré, in early September 2005. Hurricane Katrina had swept across New Orleans, southeastern Louisiana, and southern Mississippi. The monster storm shredded the Mississippi coast, and levee failures submerged much of New Orleans. The chaos and human suffering were beyond anything any of us had witnessed on American soil in our lifetimes.

I was communications director for then-Governor Kathleen Blanco of Louisiana. For days, we had begged the White House, the Federal Emergency Management Agency (FEMA) and other federal agencies for all the help and resources they could provide. In the beginning, at least, Washington did little. Blanco had called up every available National Guard member in Louisiana (thousands of our Guardsmen were in Iraq at the time). But with the New Orleans Police Department shattered and scattered, the situation was deteriorating fast. We needed boots on the ground – and quick.

That's when Gen. Honoré showed up, and, for the first time that week, I felt some hope that the tide might turn. As commander of Joint Task Force Katrina, he was in charge of some 20,000 troops, 200 rescue helicopters and 20 ships.

When he arrived at the state's Emergency Operations Center in Baton Rouge, it was obvious that this was a man accustomed to and not flustered by chaos. I doubt he knew exactly what he would find in New Orleans and precisely what he would do, but it was clear in his voice and manner that there was little he and his soldiers couldn't handle.

Day after day, those around him began to hear the now-famous lines:

"Don't get stuck on stupid" or "We're stuck on stupid!"

It was a simple but powerful message: We're not going to solve our problems by applying the same failed remedies. He was saying, in effect, "Let's re-examine the situation, be honest about the causes, and be smart and courageous in applying the right solutions."

In the weeks that followed, as his troops helped restore order and sanity to New Orleans and the surrounding area, America saw in General Honoré what so many of us have admired for years: clear-headedness, an innate ability to size up a situation quickly, a willingness to directly and honestly identify critical problems, the courage to speak truth to power, and leadership qualities that reassure and inspire those around him.

This native son of Louisiana not only helped turn the tide in New Orleans. Later, he returned to his beloved state in retirement to form and lead another division, a collection of environmental groups known as the "Green Army." As he did after Katrina, General Honoré is working to rescue his state by giving voice to those whose homes and communities have been fouled by oil and chemical companies that the state and federal government have failed to regulate adequately.

His message is so clear that it's hard to believe we have missed it over the years: No state or country will solve its chronic problems – education, crime, the environment – if it will not stand back, honestly appraise the situation, re-think its failed policies, rely upon solid research and consult those with the most experience in dealing with the issues at hand.

In other words, continuing to do the same thing again and again is stupid. Some observers might couch their criticism of failed policies in more diplomatic terms. General Honoré understands, however, that sometimes we need blunt words to wake us up and force us to look at a situation with new eyes.

That's what he has done with this book. In these pages, Russel Honoré is pointing to the stupid ways we ignore or wrongly address some of society's most vexing problems. In his distinctive style, he doesn't hesitate to speak blunt truths about where we are screwing up and what we must do about it. If you're outraged about the inability of our leaders to solve (or even recognize) our most serious problems and don't know where to turn, this book is an excellent place to start.

– Robert Mann
  Manship Chair in Journalism
  Manship School of Mass Communication
  Louisiana State University

CONTENTS

DON'T GET STUCK ON STUPID!

Chapter 1

Don't get stuck on stupid!
(Or, let's find better ways to solve our problems)

Life is tough, but it's tougher when you're stupid.

– John Wayne

Many people who keep up with current events think I'm the one who coined the phrase, "Don't get stuck on stupid!"

But I'm not the guy. It wasn't me. This little gem has been a part of American street language for a long time.

While I didn't invent the phrase, it is something I'm known for having said during a particularly stressful time in the Gulf Coast hurricane season.

The story behind it began on the Saturday before Hurricane Katrina hit New Orleans in August of 2005, while the powerful storm was churning in the Caribbean. I was at my headquarters, at Fort Gillem in Atlanta, and we had a video conference with Northern Command and the White House.

President George W. Bush had talked to people in charge of the National Hurricane Center, who told him this was going to be a bad storm and that he'd better get ready to send in the troops. The President shared that message with us while we were preparing to head for the Gulf Coast.

As part of the military's preparation for the storm, we were deploying our forward assets along the coast in Mississippi and Alabama. I remembered the first rule of warfare from Napoleon is that you've got to get there – got to go where the action is, or will be. Some of Napoleon's victories were the result of his surprising the enemy by getting there when they thought he couldn't.

I felt it was the same for dealing with hurricanes. We wanted to deploy as soon as possible, but we were being told only to "get ready" to go into the area that was likely to be most affected. My staff and I were frustrated, because we felt we needed to be where the hurricane was going to hit.

All those things were stirring in my head when I drove back home to Fort McPherson. I started pulling weeds in my garden to keep my mind busy and to think about strategy. I also had the radio playing in my truck. It was on a blues station out of Atlanta, and they started to play "Stuck on Stupid" by Shirley Brown.

I sat in my truck, lit a cigar and listened to that catchy little tune. You know how sometimes a song will hit you, and you find yourself humming to it? All through the weekend, that song stayed in my head:

I'd have to be silly,
I'd have to really be a fool ...
I'd have to be stuck on stupid!

At some point, it hit me. It was an *Ah, ha!* moment. I was being "stuck on stupid" because I was fighting the last war, battling the last hurricane. First of all, we did not have orders deploying us toward the hurricane. Secondly, Katrina's projected path was northward toward Birmingham and Atlanta and would cross our ground deployment route. We had to avoid old mistakes, and we had to make better choices and find better solutions.

After a while, I realized it made a lot of sense to wait to deploy. The winds were too high to travel on the Interstate and too strong to fly. As a first responder, you have to work hard not to be a victim yourself. Because if you're a victim, you're not going to be able to help anybody.

As the hours passed, though, people were looking for us to come to the rescue of New Orleans like the cavalry, but we couldn't move until it was safe. Once we got there, we heard the same anxious question many times:

"Why didn't you get here sooner?"

The answer was simple. To move toward the storm would be counter-productive. If we were in the

President George W. Bush listens as I update him on the impact of Hurricane Rita, shortly after his arrival in Lake Charles, La., on Sept. 27, 2005. Walking with us are Lake Charles Mayor Randy Roach (left) and U.S. Coast Guard Vice Admiral Thad Allen (right).

storm's path, we'd be victims along with everyone else. We'd be fighting the storm and battling to keep order, instead of getting there when we were needed.

About three weeks later, with New Orleans getting under control after Katrina, we were faced with another hurricane, Rita. This one was headed for the Louisiana-Texas border area, and we moved quickly in that direction. Different hurricane, different situation.

While preparing for Rita, we were conducting a news conference, and a young reporter named Rick Leventhal – who later became my friend – kept aggressively asking us why we didn't do the same thing for Katrina. I told him that the purpose of this news conference was to explain what we were going to do about the new storm that was coming our way – not to explain why we didn't do things differently for the last storm.

"We're not stuck on stupid! Why talk about Hurricane Katrina when we've got Hurricane Rita in the Gulf?" I said.

He waited a minute, then he came right back with the same question.

"You're stuck on stupid!" I told him.

We were trying to prepare for the future storm with little time to spare, but he wanted to waste precious minutes hashing out the storm that had already passed.

Naturally, the news conference was being carried live on the cable networks. So, this is when many in the general public started associating me with the catchphrase, "Don't get stuck on stupid!"

*   *   *

A couple months later, in November of 2005, I attended a state dinner for Prince Charles at the White House. Before I could even introduce myself to him, Prince Charles recognized me from the Katrina operation and commented:

"I really like that term, 'Don't get stuck on stupid,' General," he said with a half-smile.

Now, I don't know if literally everyone I meet

connects me to that phrase, but I will say I always try to live my life in keeping with the principle it suggests. So, when I'm making decisions I try to avoid the same old mistakes I've made in the past; I look for better, more effective ways to solve the problem or meet the challenge.

• Are we doing the *right* thing – or are we choosing the easier wrong over the harder right?

• Is this done based on science and sustainability, or is it based on some partisanship ideal, religious belief or demagoguery?

• Does it have an economic interest or profit motive for somebody who's driving this decision?

In the United States, it's not just our response to hurricanes that's sometimes "stuck on stupid," of course. We see it everywhere, from schools to prisons, from environmental policies to healthcare, and from businesses to guns. My goal is to call out the stupid, to face reality, and to offer solutions – even if it means speaking the unspeakable.

Chapter 2

A surefire antidote to stupidity: Great leadership

We are all born ignorant, but one must work hard to remain stupid.

– Benjamin Franklin

On November 22, 1963, I was a junior at Rosenwald High School in New Roads, Louisiana, when we got the shock of our lives. The announcement came over the intercom:

"President Kennedy has been shot."

The next thing that happened was silence. We sat there for several minutes and nobody said a word. Then the handkerchiefs came out and people started crying.

That group of kids in that segregated classroom believed that John F. Kennedy was a voice to create change and that he would allow us to live up to our potential. We were starting to believe Martin

Great leaders

Some of the most notable leaders in world history have been U.S. presidents.

George Washington   Abraham Lincoln

Luther King Jr.'s words that we would be judged by our character and our contributions, and not by the color of our skin.

America was changing, and then this happened.

What went through the minds of us kids in that classroom – and in classrooms and homes and businesses across the nation – were deeply troubling questions.

Did they kill him to punish us?

Did they kill him to prevent the advancement of people like us that he had started talking about?

What happens now?

We recognized President Kennedy as a true leader who was starting conversations about equality that resonated with our minority community and offered us hope for the future. People don't like to change, but leaders demand change.

George Washington successfully led our battle for freedom from the British. Abraham Lincoln successfully led the country through devastating internal fights of the Civil War. In our lifetime, John Kennedy

Dwight Eisenhower   John Kennedy

was taking on the seemingly impossible task of transitioning us into the next great cultural shift: integration. He was about to change the nation.

And then they killed him.

Three traits of great leaders

There are three traits that all great leaders like Kennedy, Washington and Lincoln shared. First, they did the routine things well. Second, they achieved what others thought of as impossible. And third, they were not afraid of criticism.

In the Army, we described the attributes of a good leader as "Be-Know-Do." *Be* where you are supposed to be and with whom you are supposed to be. *Know* your craft. Then *do* it.

This is simple enough, and it's the bare minimum for good leadership. But how do we recognize a *great* leader who's mastered more than the bare minimum and who's taken the art and science of leadership to a new level? And how can we improve our own skills to become better leaders?

To begin with, great leaders have a way of making their purpose known. They will pause to remember the lessons from past experiences and from the great leaders who influenced them, and they will lean on those experiences to make decisions.

You can always tell a great leader by what people do when the leader is not there. It's telling when someone says, "If the boss was here, what would she do?" It's sort of like the Jesus question, "What would Jesus do?" – WWJD?

We can also judge a great leader by how well the organization or team functions without that person. A great leader doesn't build the organization or team to run only when he or she is present; things should run as effectively whether the leader is there or not.

What's more, great leaders don't demand that people respect them. On the contrary, people go out of their way wanting to respect a great leader. Great leaders *command* respect; they don't *demand* it. And this is a very big difference.

The definition of leadership

For most of my 37 years in the Army, we considered **leadership** to be *the art and science of influencing others to perform a task or accomplish a mission.* It was only when I was about to retire from the Army that I realized we were missing a key word, "*willingly.*"

People willingly do something because they've bought in to the task or mission and they feel they are a part of that task or mission. Great leaders understand this and they create an environment where others are eager to follow. They motivate people to want to be there – and to perform to the best of their abilities. This is true for any leader in any situation – in the Army, in business, in sports or in the family at home.

In the Army, good leaders struggle with trying to balance what's more important: Our people or our mission. Great leaders don't struggle with this, because the people and the mission are equally important. Great leaders challenge the men and women in their command, they have a sense of appreciation for those around them, and they have a way of leading without favoritism.

If you think back to your high school and college days, the best teachers and professors didn't walk into the room and announce, "I'm a leader! Pay attention to me!" Instead, they walked into the room with a distinct presence. And you behaved in class because you respected the teacher and looked forward to hearing what she or he had to say.

The best teachers – like the best generals, the best company presidents and the best parents – have a way of motivating you to do your best. Respect is a two-way street. You have to respect and trust those under your leadership if you are to earn their respect and trust in return.

It's 'impossible' only because it hasn't been done before

Two of the great leaders from American history were George Washington and Abraham Lincoln. Each fought a war in his own country – the American Revolution and the Civil War, respectively.

These men were by no means perfect, but they were the right people at the right time – and there was a level of greatness in both of them that transcended their flaws and frailties. Washington himself owned slaves and he wasn't a standout on the battlefield. He was just an average guy, but he had aspirations to be as good as the great men surrounding him, like John Adams and Thomas Jefferson. And he achieved the first great transformation of American history by winning our independence from the British in a daring and decisive military victory.

Washington didn't have the proper supplies, he barely had an army, and he didn't have artillery. But he led his men into battle against the British by using every trick in the book. Who would have believed that his ragtag army could beat the most powerful army in the world? It just seemed impossible, because Washington's army was made up of a militia and a few federal troops, plus farmers, bricklayers, carpenters and masons who left their jobs to go to war.

The advantage Washington had was that his men believed in him and they also believed in the cause of independence.

The British army was made up of mercenaries

and draftees. It didn't matter that they had the best weapons and the best generals, because our ancestors fought for freedom and the British troops fought only for a king – King George III. The British weren't following a great leader; they were following an ideology. But it wasn't their own ideology, it was someone else's, so they were not fully committed to their cause.

Washington's greatest triumph was the Battle of Trenton in late 1776. The United States capital in New York had been destroyed, and the British were positioned to cross the Delaware River from New Jersey into Pennsylvania to capture the temporary capital in Philadelphia.

Washington had only about 2,400 troops remaining, and the British knew those troops were demoralized and were marching without adequate food, clothing and weaponry. To make matters worse, they were trapped in the midst of a bitter winter.

The last thing the British expected was for Washington to attack them, especially on Christmas Day. At sunset on Christmas Day, though, Washington led his troops across the freezing Delaware River from Pennsylvania, using boats he borrowed from local fishermen. Many of his men didn't have boots or coats.

They took the British by surprise at Trenton. About 1,000 British soldiers were killed, injured, or captured, while only two of Washington's men were killed and five were injured.

Washington achieved the impossible, even though he was not sure he would succeed. Yes, he was afraid, but he wasn't afraid to fail and he wasn't afraid to face criticism for trying.

Two days before he crossed the Delaware River, Washington made sure that every man under his command heard *The Crisis*, an essay written by his friend and fellow patriot Thomas Paine. Most of the troops couldn't read, but Washington wanted to share something that would inspire them. The essay starts with the immortal words, "These are the times that try men's souls." *The Crisis* served as a rousing battle cry. Washington's men were deeply motivated to continue fighting for their own independence and freedom.

*   *   *

Lincoln lived a hard life. It's not like he strolled over to the Ritz-Carlton one day and said, "I'm going to run for President." He literally came out of a log cabin in the backwoods and worked his way up through political influence to become President at one of the most volatile times in our history. This is so American. It's the story of our nation.

Lincoln died young, but he also transformed the country through his decisive leadership. He fought the Civil War to keep the United States intact and to preserve the vision of the Founding Fathers, even though it meant brother fighting brother and

The Crisis

By Thomas Paine

These are the times that try men's souls.

The summer soldier and the sunshine patriot will, in this crisis, shrink from the service of their country; but he that stands by it now deserves the love and thanks of man and woman.

Tyranny, like hell, is not easily conquered; yet we have this consolation with us, that the harder the conflict, the more glorious the triumph. What we obtain too cheap, we esteem too lightly: It is dearness only that gives every thing its value. Heaven knows how to put a proper price upon its goods; and it would be strange indeed if so celestial an article as freedom should not be highly rated.

families being ripped apart by vicious political and philosophical divisions.

Although he was a committed abolitionist, he was conflicted over the merits of freeing the slaves at that time. Through a lot of reflection and introspection, however, he raised the debate above himself and looked at what he felt was best for the nation. That is a mark of great leadership. Like Kennedy a century later, Lincoln was not afraid to strive for the seemingly impossible, and he was willing to face criticism to defend what he believed was both morally right and in the nation's best interest.

On January 1, 1863, Lincoln issued the Emancipation Proclamation, which led to the Thirteenth Amendment, abolishing slavery in 1865.

History is full of similar examples of bravery and great leadership. The D-Day invasion at Normandy, France, on June 6, 1944, is another example of what can happen when great leaders ask for the impossible. General Dwight D. Eisenhower achieved the nearly unachievable by attacking the seemingly unassailable German positions at Normandy and forcing the Germans to retreat. It was the beginning of the end of World War II.

D-Day was the greatest amphibious landing in history. It required more than 5,000 boats and 13,000 aircraft to send more than 160,000 Allied troops across the English Channel from England to France, all the while battling the Germans. The Allies suffered about 10,000 casualties, including

Allied troops storm the beaches of Normandy, France, on D-Day, June 6, 1944. The bold decision to attack the well-entrenched Germans at this point marked the beginning of the end of World War II.

more than 4,400 men who were killed.

When the very fate of the free world was on the line, Eisenhower showed levels of courage and leadership that we rarely see. Nothing like the D-Day invasion had ever been done before, so it took bold action and a belief that only by doing the impossible could we change the course of history. The lessons of D-Day stand as a supreme example that change always comes with a risk of failure – and that great leaders are not afraid to make that sacrifice and to do what nearly everyone would consider impossible.

*   *   *

'Soldiers will not follow any battle leader with confidence unless they know that he will require full performance of duty from every member of the team.'

– Gen. Dwight D. Eisenhower

I met one of the greatest leaders I ever knew in 1973, when I was a lieutenant in the 2nd Infantry Division in South Korea. Henry E. Emerson was a three-star general who wore a cowboy hat and carried pearl-handled pistols while in uniform. I'd never seen anything like this in my life, but he related with the troops. He was phenomenal.

Emerson was bigger than life, and he coined the phrase "Fight tonight!" When you saluted him as a soldier, you would say "Second to none, sir," and he would return your salute with "Fight tonight!"

We were in a volatile part of the world, and everyone knew an attack from North Korea could come at night because it would give them cover from our aircraft. "Fight tonight!" was a reminder that we always had to be ready. Emerson knew how to motivate his men, and he knew they would follow him willingly into the fight because he was a great leader.

If we're not changing, we're falling behind
When I took charge of the First Army as

Commanding General in June of 2004, we had eight camps where we trained soldiers to fight in Iraq and Afghanistan. I asked the colonels to explain to me what they were doing, and the typical conversation went something like this:

"Well, sir, we are training the units on what they want to be trained on."

"That's interesting," I said, "but how do they know what training they need?"

"From the last unit they are replacing, sir."

That didn't sound right to me. We were treating our soldiers like they were our customers telling us what they wanted.

After a few of these conversations, I said we were going to start training people the way they were going to fight in Iraq and Afghanistan. Within days, that became the catch phrase of the people in command:

"We're going to train them the way they are going to fight."

Every private and every colonel in that regiment became focused on their missions.

The First Army remains committed to that ideal: Train like you are going to fight. It's a lesson that extends to every level of leadership, because you have to do the routine things well – but you also have to adapt to changing conditions.

The leaders – in the Army, in business, at school, or at home – must inspire the people under their command to prepare to meet greater challenges, whether it's fighting in Iraq or Afghanistan, making innovative business decisions, or taking a more advanced class.

Patriots don't always wear uniforms

The idea of patriotism is often associated with those in uniform. We need to draw that back, however, because patriotism is an obligation of *all* citizens, not just those serving in the military.

It doesn't matter where you live, you are part of the bigger tribe of your community – whether you associate that tribe with your neighborhood, your city, your state or your nation. Whatever it is, we all share a common bond that we must be willing to protect.

Brigadier General James "Robbie" Risner was a prisoner of war in Vietnam, and when he came home, he wrote and spoke about patriotism and service.

First, he said that we are all born free by accident. It has nothing to do with anything we did but is based only on the time and place of our birth – "an accident of birth." And, of course, we must recognize that not everyone is born free.

Second, he said to live free is a privilege that was paid for by those who preceded us. It's not just those who fought in wars or the more than 2.6 million Americans who were killed and injured in wars, from the American Revolution to the war on terror.

Just as important are those who stayed back home to take care of the family or raise the food or make the equipment used in battle. These people were all part of the team. Teachers, engineers, shopkeepers and even politicians all did their parts to ensure our freedom today.

Third, Risner said that to die free is an obligation. The average age of the 10,000 casualties on D-Day was 25 and under. You are talking about some serious sacrifice here. Living free is a great privilege, and each generation has an obligation to defend that freedom for future generations.

It's incumbent on all of us to teach our children that regardless of what happens, we must pass along freedom to the next generation. We don't ever want to be so complacent that we would put our freedom at risk because we are reluctant to stand up to fight for it.

* * *

Many who fought for our country in the armed forces were not fully appreciated for their service nor shown the respect they deserved. But they served anyway.

In World War I, the Harlem Hellfighters was an African American infantry regiment that was shunned by the U.S. Congress but fought with distinction in French uniforms; in World War II, Japanese Americans fought in the U.S. Army despite the fact that as many as 120,000 of them were held in American internment camps; and in both world wars, Native Americans joined the Army and developed unbreak-

The Harlem Hellfighters, an African American regiment who fought in World War I, are among the minority groups who served in foreign wars on behalf of the U.S. throughout the 20th century.

able codes based on their native languages, even though the U.S. had a shameful history of killing their ancestors.

These patriotic Americans were not treated with fairness when they came back home. Many were not allowed to enjoy the very freedoms for which they had put their lives on the line. They had to fight another fight: They could not eat in the same restaurants as white citizens or drink from the same water fountains or attend the same schools. Voting was all but impossible for them in many places.

*   *   *

Great leaders inspire patriotism. They inspire participation in our democracy, but they also teach, heal and lead through example for the greater good of the community.

The stupid thing is that too often we follow bad leaders who rise to the top through wealth, intimidation and/or false promises. We must learn to recognize great leaders and let them become examples for our own behavior and our own brand of leadership.

Great leadership is the best way to defeat stupidity.

—— *Calls to action* ——

1. Vote.

2. Run for office.

3. Organize and demonstrate when something is wrong.

4. Volunteer and give to your community.

5. Follow the examples of great leaders.

6. Don't keep making the same mistakes ... don't get stuck on stupid!

Chapter 3

Politics, power and public service

*In politics, stupidity
is not a handicap.*

– Napoleon Bonaparte

The Italian economic historian Carlo M. Cipolla defined a "stupid person" as one who makes decisions that harm himself and others. He also called a person a "bandit" who benefits himself while harming others.

Another word for both "stupid person" and "bandit" would be, in many cases, "politician."

Since I retired from the Army, people often ask me if I would consider running for the governorship of Louisiana. After all, when you achieve a certain level of notoriety, people expect more from you.

Many of the people who ask me this question aren't interested in how I would govern or in my opinions about schools, healthcare, prisons, the environment, the budget deficit or any of the dozens of other problems facing our state.

Instead, they want to know the answers to only two questions:

"Are you gonna take my guns away?"

"Where do you stand on abortion?"

I have eight guns and, of course, I don't believe in killing babies, but that's usually not enough to satisfy anyone who asks the questions. Anyone who's seen political ads on TV knows that a disproportionate amount of time and money are spent on trying to define an opponent on single issues like guns and abortion.

But we've got many issues to deal with as a state and as a nation.

And on the question of my running for governor, I didn't run largely because I felt I could be more effective from the outside than from the inside.

*   *   *

The real art of political leadership is to reduce complex issues to simpler terms so that people can understand them. It is also the ability to solve problems economically, legally and diplomatically. In contrast, politics today is often led by selfish people with a degree of power who are guided by people with money and influence who want more money and more influence.

We have to keep reminding ourselves that our

democracy is still taking shape. If it isn't still taking shape, then why do women make only 80 cents for every dollar a man makes? Why do African Americans earn less than 75 cents for every dollar earned by whites? Why is there inequity in our school systems when we all pay the same taxes and all live in the same place?

What sets us apart as Americans, though, is that we have the ability to talk about these issues and confront our leaders. Freedom of speech is guaranteed in the First Amendment to the Constitution.

Unfortunately, we also have a proclivity for stupidity. For example, Louisiana, like many other states, has become what amounts to a single-party state. We were always divided, but in any given political cycle in the past, we could have a Democratic or Republican majority. Then it went red and stayed red. It's like we got permanently stupid – not *because* the state went red, but because with one-party rule there is little incentive to change or innovate.

Instead of segregated schools, we have at least five different school systems in Louisiana. Our education is worse, not better. We put more people in prison than any other state. And our sales tax is the highest in the nation.

Which brings up the question about why we keep electing the same politicians who don't solve problems but keep adding to them.

Too many politicians don't understand the old saying "You can fool all the people some of the time, and some of the people all the time, but you cannot fool all the people all the time." They're good enough at getting elected, but they have no idea about leadership and compassion toward their people. For them, the ends justify the means.

However, there is always a willing press standing by to tell the people just how stupid their politicians are. The freedom of the press to challenge the government is written into the Constitution. It assures us that "we the people" have access to the workings of government and that politicians are held accountable to the people. Without this balance, the politicians could fool all the people all the time – as they do in authoritarian regimes in which the government controls the press.

A democracy that is not transparent through the media is not a true democracy.

A new world is created every three months

Maybe we ought to give politicians a pass on campaign promises. When they get elected, they should start over. They should find out what's going on, then come back with real solutions. They have to switch from being politicians who appeal only to their base supporters, to being responsible public servants who represent all the people.

Plus, the world changes. Bill Gates once said that in his world at Microsoft, things change so rapidly that his company doesn't work in traditional 12-month years. They essentially start a new year every three months.

It should be the same in politics. Let's stop being stupid. From the day you win the Presidency until the time you get into office, that's a year in Bill Gates' terms. The world doesn't stop, and if you don't change along with it, you will look stupid. The things that helped get you elected are not the same things that sustain you once elected. Campaign promises may sound good, but once in office, it's never as easy to get anything done as we were led to believe.

President Barack Obama promised to close Gitmo – the U.S. military prison at Guantanamo Bay Naval Station in Cuba – but he discovered it really wasn't his decision, and it's still not closed. He also promised to reduce the number of troops on the ground overseas, and he did that. But then we had to send our troops back into Afghanistan, and our people are still chasing ISIS around the Middle East.

President Bill Clinton had a "reinvestment" plan that reduced the size of the military and put the money back into communities across America. It was a campaign promise that might have sounded good, but it nearly killed the Army.

When we came out of Desert Storm, we had a smaller military, and a lot of bases were closed as a result. Our budget was cut so much that we were doing crazy stuff like using golf carts to practice for driving tanks. We had to limit the number of hours and miles our tanks would run in a year, but how can anyone get proficient in a tank when he's allowed to drive only one hour a month?

You just never know how things will work out, and it should alarm us that a President or other politician wouldn't adapt his or her position to a changing world. Altering your position on a topic once you fully understand it is not a sign of weakness. On the contrary, it is a sign of strength and leadership.

The three main types of government

There are **three basic kinds of government**, determined by the amount of authority held by the officials, elected or otherwise.

The first is an **authoritarian government**, in which the power lies in a single ruler or a few people at the top. There isn't much of this kind of government left these days anywhere in the world, and people don't like it because there is no freedom of speech and they have no power. The most obvious example today is North Korea, but China and Cuba are also run by authoritarian governments, and Russia is borderline.

The second type is a **constitutional monarchy**. Kings once ruled with absolute power, but almost every remaining monarchy has been reined in with a constitution that spells out the rights and responsibilities of the monarch. A royal family, such as the ones in the United Kingdom and Belgium, has little power, but it is there to christen ships and to show up on ceremonial occasions.

Then there is what we have in the United States, a **democracy** in which citizens vote for what they want or do it through the representatives they elect. In theory, the power is retained by the people.

In our democracy, if something happens to the President, we have a Vice President who takes over, not a son or a son-in-law or a brother. When the Vice President takes over, he cleans house, so the system ends up being bigger than any President. That's what keeps the political balance in America.

Things get murky with our democracy, though, because there are lobbyists standing between the citizens and the people they elect to carry out their wishes. These interest groups get decisively engaged in politics. We have too many situations in which groups like the National Rifle Association have a powerful influence on government and can get laws and regulations passed that are not always in the best interest of the public at large.

Almost every day, you can read in the newspaper or hear a story on television about a lobbying campaign that succeeded in getting legislation passed or stopped. Often, the reason for the success is not the will of the people but the will – or, more specifically, the money – of the lobbyists.

At the same time, we've got a population that has become disinterested in one of the most valuable attributes our forebears won for us when our nation was founded: The right to vote. In 1960, about 63 percent of the population voted in the Presidential election; it was less than 50 percent in 1996, and it's been around 55 percent since then.

What this means is that nearly half the eligible voters don't bother voting for President, and when it comes to low-profile elections like city council and ballot measures, the turnout can be as low as 20 percent or even in the single digits.

The four elements of power

For a time during my military career, I operated at the highest levels of national government. As Vice Director for Operations on the Joint Chiefs of Staff during the Clinton administration, I was in the Situation Room for meetings of the White House National Security Council, which is the principal interagency body that advises the President on national security and foreign policy matters.

What I discovered in high-level meetings like this is that there are four elements of power: legal, economic, diplomatic and military.

In one meeting, the State Department representative leaned across the table during a discussion about possible military intervention in Kosovo. She noted that military action might be the most expedient answer to our immediate problems, but it might not be the best thing because it would not secure a long-term solution.

All options were seriously considered before any action was taken, with the clear understanding that military action generally happens only when diplomacy fails. When you use weapons, it's consequential, because enemies can shoot back. It also has to be part of an overall strategy that takes into account the other elements of power.

Effective politicians have to take the long-term view rather than the easiest route with short-term gains. In contrast, ineffective politicians make snap judgments without considering the four elements of power.

When President Donald Trump ordered a military strike on an airfield in Syria in 2017, he supposedly ordered the strike only after his daughter showed him photographs of the carnage caused by chemical weapons attacks that were reportedly carried out by that nation's President against his own people. Pictures of dead babies really upset him.

While the Syrian strike itself was impressive in the accuracy and effectiveness of the 59 Tomahawk cruise missiles fired from warships in the Mediterranean Sea, it's not clear whether Trump considered the other elements of power before ordering the military option. Having been in on meetings where similar things were discussed, I didn't get the impression there was a strategy beyond simply bombing the airfield.

If you bomb an airfield in Syria, what is the overall goal? Is it regime change to overthrow the elected president? Or is it to weaken him to a point where we end up with a Sunni part of the nation and a Shia part, each of which is separately governed, possibly with ISIS in the middle?

In the north of Syria near the Turkish border are the Kurds, who are keenly aware that the Syrian president was willing to slaughter his own people to achieve his political goals. He also had the backing of the Russian president, who probably had an interest in gaining access to a deepwater Mediterranean port.

Because of the four elements of power – legal, economic, diplomatic and military – the end goal can never be just bombing an airfield. There are a lot of cross-interests.

In the case of Syria, the news reports didn't help. The media immediately accepted the report that chemical weapons were used, before the government could verify it. After the bombing happened, everybody was praising it instead of analyzing what else we could have done.

We could have employed a no-fly zone. We could have blocked Syrian ports to stop their ability to do commerce. We could have withdrawn diplomatic contacts. Only if those remedies failed should military action have been necessary.

As it was, it appears that only the military option was employed and the bombing appeared to have been used to spin political points of view.

Along these lines, another possibility is that this was a case of "wag the dog" – staging a few high-profile events with almost no chance of failure to give the impression the administration was taking decisive action. In reality, the events were coordinated to distract from other failings.

Eight days after the Syria bombing, the "Mother of all Bombs" (MOAB) was dropped on a location in Afghanistan. The bomb was the most powerful non-nuclear weapon ever used, assuring it would dominate the headlines for days.

The intersection of politics and war

One of the unanswered questions of the modern world is why we are so interested in the Middle East. Until we needed oil and became gas-guzzlers, there was very little concern about what happened on the Arabian Peninsula and in the Middle East. The United States is now energy-independent, but we're still messing around over there because many of our friends depend on that oil.

People make the assumption that Desert Storm and the Gulf War were fought over oil, but that is not entirely true, because we've got more oil in the United States than we know what to do with. It was not fought strictly over oil, but it was fought to have access to oil and to keep the price low not only for us but for our European partners. So, it was more about not disrupting the market and securing oil links than it was about Saddam Hussein being a threat to America.

The companies that own the oil are multi-national. While we were in Iraq for Desert Storm and the Iraq War, from 2003 to 2011, British Petroleum (BP) delivered our fuel. They are one of the largest exporters of oil and gas in the world. What's more, the British State-run retirement system is funded partially by BP and Shell Oil Co. stock – so if BP and/or Shell stocks fail, the British government has a huge problem.

In 2010, the BP Deepwater Horizon oil well exploded

in the Gulf of Mexico and spilled millions of barrels of oil into the Gulf. There were a lot of political factors in play in the aftermath of the oil spill.

The White House sent messages that we had to be hard on BP for their environmental negligence, but that we couldn't let them fail because the corporation needed to remain solvent for the sake of the British retirement system, among other things. It appeared that our own politicians had taken so much money from BP that they were swayed to go easy on them.

As a result, the State of Louisiana's lawyers settled for a fraction of what they should have received to deal with the environmental disaster, even though they had BP over a barrel. The next thing the government allowed was for BP to pay the fine over 15 years, so they could protect their bottom line by taking tax write-offs.

The day after the settlement, BP stock went up, because it was understood that if they were charged the maximum fine and had to pay it out in one year they would have lost a lot of their North American holdings.

This is the real world of politics. It also shows how fragile a government can be and how complex the whole geo-political system can be. It's not as simple as the commentators make it seem when they speak on TV for two minutes.

* * *

I spent a good portion of my military career in Asia,

and I often get asked whether a missile strike or some other action will draw us into more of a continuing conflict in that part of the world. Most of my adult life, we've been involved in the Middle East, so it's unlikely anything will change as a result of one isolated event.

When you're dealing with the Middle East in particular, politics is never far away, and it's extremely complex.

The picture that politicians like to paint is that people in the Middle East want to come over here and destroy our country. In reality, the majority of people have no desire other than to do what they are already doing. They are just going about their business, and they want to work and have a safe place to raise their families in peace.

I've gone all over the world, and it's the same everywhere. I've been out in the Saudi desert where nobody speaks English, and the next thing you know the Bedouins are inviting me into their tent and laughing and making me a cup of tea. I've seen the same thing in South Korea, Yemen, Cuba and elsewhere.

* * *

For much of the 20th century, we devoted our military efforts and our national treasures to defending Europe and keeping the different European nations from fighting one another. We spent two world wars fighting over there, and there hasn't been another war there since the end of World War II in 1945.

This wasn't entirely a military solution; it was as much a political solution.

The last major military event in Europe was that little skirmish in Kosovo in 1998 and 1999. It wasn't an all-out war situation, but we solved it because we were there. We had 250,000 troops in Europe until after Desert Storm, and at one time we had half a million troops over there. I spent six years in Europe myself.

It took many years, but thanks to a political and military strategy, we have celebrated the longest period of peace in recorded history in Europe. It goes to show that we can't become too impatient.

However, we need to make up our minds about what we're trying to do in the Middle East. The focus shifts constantly and we keep supporting different groups. In Iraq, we ran off the Sunnis and now it's run by Shias, but those people hate each other. In Syria, which is run by Shias, we want to put Sunnis in charge.

It's fundamentally messed up. To be successful, we need to have a long-term strategy and we need to figure out which side we are going to support.

We have spent trillions of dollars in Iraq and we have seen more than 4,400 U.S. troops killed and about 32,000 injured, and we may end up with Iraq being aligned with Iran. This is not what we had in mind when we went into the Gulf War and the Iraq War.

The cost to win
and hold public office

One of the biggest things we see in politics is that the higher you go, the more money it takes to stay there and to move up. Money is a huge problem, because it costs so much to run for office – and that makes politicians vulnerable to those with money who can help them stay in power. As soon as one election is over, the politicians are already campaigning and raising money for the next election.

The average cost of winning a seat in the U.S. House of Representatives is about $1.7 million. In the U.S. Senate, it is about $10.5 million, which requires a sitting Senator to raise nearly $5,000 every day of a six-year term.

The legendary Louisiana Governor and U.S. Senator Huey Long said it best when he noted that the three most important things to a politician are getting re-elected, getting re-elected, and getting re-elected. Nothing has changed since the 1930s.

When regulators hang out at night with the people they're supposed to be regulating, you know you've got trouble. And when lobbyists donate millions of dollars to politicians and then get legislation that favors them and not the general public, there's a good chance the politicians were swayed by the cash and not by the voters.

* * *

One of the biggest strengths of our democracy is that since our people can read and can share information on social media, when they realize something's wrong or needs to be changed, they are going to raise hell. It doesn't matter who is in the White House.

Fighting back against the ingrained political system is much more effective when we have an active constituency who can organize, use social media, send out newsletters and write op-eds for local newspapers.

Our least effective communities are the ones that can't do that – and they are mostly poor communities that need the most help. People who live in poverty have less means to deal with problems and raise consciousness.

However, when people get worried and ask me how things will work out, I say it's going to work out fine. We've survived a lot worse than what's happening today, and we have the advantage of being able to study thousands of years of history and politics.

We know a lot more today than our ancestors did, but the political game hasn't changed much. It's a good thing we don't take Presidents and politicians as seriously as they take themselves, because it would drive us all crazy. We know we live in a world where we have little power over what goes on in the big picture, and to think otherwise is naive. Tomorrow, Mother Nature could flood this place, or some idiot could start a war somewhere.

As long as we have three functioning branches of government and a functioning media, we may become bent, but we won't break. I love my country and the place where I live, but there's a lot of work still to be done. It ain't always pretty, but on any given day it's better than any alternative.

Democracy will always win.

—— *Calls to action* ——

1. Consider all options before making a decision.

2. Fight back against anything that seems unjust.

3. Follow the money in politics and hold everyone accountable.

4. Support the free press.

5. Vote in every election. Your voice counts!

6. Don't keep making the same mistakes ... don't get stuck on stupid!

The 2017 hurricane season brought extraordinary damage to Texas, Florida and Puerto Rico. **Above:** Homes, businesses and the power grid were mauled by high winds as Hurricane Maria swept through Puerto Rico. **Below:** Houston residents had to be rescued from their badly flooded neighborhoods in the wake of Hurricane Harvey.

Chapter 4

Hurricanes, floods and infrastructure failure

There is nothing so stupid as the educated man if you get him off the thing he was educated in.

– Will Rogers

One of the big issues facing us in the late 20th century was the so-called Y2K problem, which was the potential for computers to go haywire when their calendars moved from 1999 to 2000. Computer codes were originally written with the year as a two-digit number, leaving off the initial "19." As the year 2000 approached, experts worried that computers would think "00" was 1900 instead of 2000 and would therefore crash because the date would be off by 100 years.

The fear was that computers running banks, airlines, and even governments would cease to function and that widespread chaos would take over. Nuclear weapons would launch by themselves, ATMs would randomly spit out $20 bills, the stock market would crash, airplanes would drop out of the sky and governments would fail!

I was in Washington at this time, and we were working on the Y2K issue. I spent December 31, 1999, at the Pentagon, watching for signs of trouble around the world. We had forward deployed troops all over the world in strategic sites, and they were ready to go. We had practiced all of the drills to protect Washington, D.C., because we didn't know what would happen.

Just like everyone else, we did a lot of work to protect all our computers and to make sure nothing happened with our nuclear arsenal. The solution, however, was fairly simple: change the year code to a four-digit number – but with so many computers and so much data, there was a possibility of missing something.

As it turned out, nothing happened, but it showed us how vulnerable we were to infrastructure failures – and that responding to a crisis takes much more effort, time and money than simply planning ahead.

A changing climate requires changing ideas

Other than Pearl Harbor in 1941 and the terrorist attacks in 2001, never before in our country's history have we faced a crisis at home that is as immediate and important as the one we face today from our crumbling and badly managed infrastructure.

But it wasn't the Russians or a terrorist network

that did this to us. We did it to ourselves by ignoring the warning signs and not making adequate preparations.

This crisis has been known about for many years, but it really became evident in the summer of 2017 when the triple hurricanes of Harvey, Irma and Maria hit Texas, Florida and Puerto Rico, respectively. Every day for several weeks on end, we turned on our televisions and checked the Internet for updates on the disasters that were unfolding in several major metropolitan areas and across the entire island of Puerto Rico.

Even after disasters like Hurricane Katrina in 2005, it's frustrating to think that planning on the ground still hasn't been implemented to avert disasters of this nature. This is something we are very capable of doing – just like we have done to improve hurricane tracking. We might be able to predict with a new level of accuracy where a hurricane may strike, but in general we are not using technology and scientific research nearly enough to help our people. It's possible to use these resources so much better, but politics and various vested interests have taken precedence over the well-being of our country.

We are at a critical point in history – not just for our national security, but for our health and safety and the future of our country. That's why it's important to take a different approach, because we can't depend only on the professionals and the politicians to make things better. In many instances, they haven't even addressed the issues in earnest. Someone needs to raise the distress flag.

If our people aren't safe, our country is vulnerable. The only one who can save us is us.

* * *

One of the greatest issues we face is that weather patterns are changing. This severely affects the way in which our houses, our neighborhoods, our cities, our states and our entire nation have to deal with such dramatic and immediate changes. This is not just a societal issue, it is a national security issue.

The weather and infrastructure may seem like separate issues, but they're well connected. If our roads and railroads, for example, are not adequate in times of emergency, large sections of the population will be in even greater danger from the floods and hurricanes that we know will be coming.

Something needs to be done to defenseless areas to mitigate problems caused by severe weather events; many of these problems were exposed by Hurricanes Harvey in Texas and Maria in Puerto Rico.

An egregious example of how we have created our own problems is that we have allowed developers to build entire neighborhoods in known floodplains – in Houston, Texas, for example. About 90 percent of all natural disasters in the United States involve flooding, so most insurers no longer offer flood insurance because it is not profitable. As a result, the National

Flood Insurance Program (NFIP) was introduced in 1968 to provide flood insurance to communities that otherwise might not be able to purchase such insurance.

The majority of the NFIP's 5.5 million policyholders are in Texas and Florida, the very states that were pummeled by hurricanes in 2017 and two of the states that are most vulnerable to climate change and rising sea levels. Before these hurricanes, the NFIP was already over $24 billion in debt, due in part to bad management and ill-conceived policies.

The NFIP debt is taxpayer money, so we're subsidizing people to build in areas that we know will flood and will need to be bailed out. That's crazy! In fact, just one percent of insured properties account for up to 30 percent of the claims and represent more than half the $24 billion debt, meaning that some properties flood multiple times and are constantly rebuilt, with our government knowing they will flood again.

More than 30,000 properties flood an average of five times every two to three years, and some properties have flooded more than 30 times. One home valued at $69,000 in California flooded 34 times in 32 years. Yet, after every flood, the NFIP rebuilt the property, spending nearly 10 times the property's value.

What's more, the average home that's flooded has a value of about $110,000 but suffers over $133,000 in flood damages – and many of these homes are rebuilt multiple times. A significant number of these homes are also vacation homes, meaning that money to help rebuild primary homes for the less wealthy is potentially being diverted. It would often be less expensive to purchase a new home in a different location than to keep rebuilding in the same location.

We know the dangers and the expenses of living in flood zones, but little is done to help people move out of them. Apart from the insane policy of rebuilding over and over again, less than two percent of the money spent on rebuilding is spent on helping people move to safer locations. Unlike a nation such as the Netherlands – much of which is below sea level but which has not experienced a major flood since 1953 – we spend more money responding to floods than preventing them.

To make matters worse – or better, if you're covered by NFIP – is the fact that the insurance policies don't increase in price, even after multiple claims for the same property. When efforts are made to increase the rates, there is a huge cry from those whose premiums would increase because they rebuild so often. Meanwhile, we the taxpayers are footing the bill and literally encouraging people to build and rebuild in places that are not sustainable for housing.

*   *   *

After a disaster, many people are clueless about how to rebuild. How many more disasters will we have to go through before things are done right?

One of the issues we see in storms such as Hurricane

Harvey is how to manage storm water. There is a normal function of the landscape and the way it deals with things such as excessive water, but that understanding has disappeared along with the natural landscapes that help the land deal with storm water.

The landscape is a huge mechanism for absorbing and purifying rainwater. Under normal circumstances, regular rains help cool the atmosphere; at the same time, the rain is soaked into the ground, where it is naturally filtered and becomes safe to drink. What we've done over the years is that we've changed this mechanism so that it is no longer functioning as it should.

Storms are ways of equalizing heat in the atmosphere, and one reason we get these huge storms now is the concentration of hot air and hot water. That's what fed the storms in Texas and Florida in 2017. The atmosphere is heating up due to the reduced amount of plant material, which increases the moisture drawn into the air and therefore the amount of water that is dropped as rain. It's a vicious cycle.

The energy in the atmosphere also plays a major role. The jet stream usually goes west to east in a fairly predictable pattern, but now it is waving up and down, more than likely due to man's influence on the atmosphere. When the jet stream goes above or around a storm, it no longer pushes it. This is contributing to more extreme weather and making the extreme weather last longer.

One of the things that rain does is slow the wind,

so with more rain we can expect slower-moving storms. We have already seen the effects of storms that sit for longer periods instead of moving along like they used to do. The floods in south Louisiana in 2016 and Hurricane Harvey in 2017 are examples of this new trend in storms.

*   *   *

Forests are one of the planet's biggest cooling mechanisms, but we have replaced great swaths of forest with lawns. The lawn is now the single largest "crop" in the United States. More lawn is grown in our country than corn or any commercial crop, and in total it covers an area about the size of Texas.

The proliferation of lawns comes at a great cost, however. It takes a tremendous amount of water to keep grass alive, and in some regions as much as 75 percent of residential water is devoted to lawns. Naturally, this puts a colossal strain on water systems. The typical lawn uses 10,000 gallons of water per year, in addition to rainwater.

Unlike trees, which absorb carbon dioxide, lawns emit considerable amounts of carbon dioxide, which contributes to the warming of the atmosphere.

The greatest harm a lawn does, however, is as a result of their being treated with chemicals. After World War II, the chemical companies led us to believe that the best lawns were bright green, weed-free and insect-free, instead of being natural.

Each year, we dump about 90 million pounds of herbicides and pesticides on our lawns, with the result that many of these chemicals are now found in groundwater. Nitrates leeching into the drinking water can have the effect, as seen in some states such as Iowa, of turning babies grey-blue (the Blue Baby Syndrome).

What all this chemical action does is alter the nature of lawns. In a natural, organic lawn or forest floor, you could have four or five inches of rain with no runoff because the water is absorbed. A chemical lawn is denser and less able to absorb water, because the chemicals undermine the biology of the soil. It becomes saturated after only an inch of rain, and the rest runs off.

In a heavy rain, a typical sewer system can usually handle only a couple of inches of rain. After that, the landscape starts to flood. In an era when we are facing heavier and more sustained rainfalls, it makes sense to return to lawns that are organic and that can handle large amounts of water – or, better yet, replace lawns with other vegetation that is not harmful to the environment.

Another issue is trees. Tree roots are being starved by lawns, again because the rain is not being absorbed adequately into the ground. Instead of lawns around trees, it's best to use other types of plant materials or no plants at all, like our grandparents used to do. Every person that owns property has the ability to contribute to the revival of healthy lawns and healthy trees, with the ultimate goal of being able to deal with storm water.

Insurance companies don't like people to have trees near their houses, because trees have a habit of falling on houses in storms. However, trees almost always fall because of bad management, not because of wind and rain. Trees are valuable, because they cool the environment, provide shade that cools houses, and break the wind. Rather than getting rid of trees, we need to understand how to maintain our trees to encourage healthy soil and healthy roots.

Infrastructure is the foundation of our society

South of the confluence of the Ohio and Mississippi rivers at Cairo, Illinois, there are just five railroad bridges crossing the Mississippi River. Known as the Lower Mississippi, this is a stretch of about 1,000 miles.

One of the reasons there are so few railroad crossings in the Lower Mississippi is that about 90 percent of all railroad freight traffic across the nation – both east-west and north-south – passes through Chicago, in the North. This makes the entire nation's railroad freight system vulnerable to a crippling weather event such as a snowstorm.

Chicago is known for its extreme winter weather, and the blizzards of 1967 and 1999 are particularly memorable. In 1999, a blizzard virtually shut down freight traffic across the nation for several weeks. Because each railroad company is privately owned and operates its own lines, they didn't coordinate their snow plowing and they were on the verge of shutting down the nation's freight system. Fortunately, the railroad companies worked out a solution by allowing train cars from one company to go from one railroad line to another.

That was an infrastructure challenge, and it was solved because people realized there was a problem and they fixed it. It didn't address the crazy situation in which 90 percent of railroad freight traffic goes through a single hub, but it was a start.

* * *

The railroads are still all privately owned, but the roads and airports across the nation are owned by various governmental entities, so we have this matrix of transportation infrastructure that is a patchwork of business and governmental bodies. And this can sometimes be a huge mess.

This is just one piece of the infrastructure jigsaw puzzle that keeps our nation running, but if any part of it fails, it could have a devastating and cumulative effect. In any community, the citizens can point to crumbling bridges, roads that are inadequate for the amount of traffic, sewer systems that need to be upgraded, school systems with inadequate facilities and so much more. As our infrastructure ages, the need to upgrade and replace it increases – and so does the cost.

Infrastructure is the foundation of our society. Without roads, bridges, schools, power plants, hospitals, communication systems and so on, our quality of life would plummet and we would become a third-world country.

Politicians tend to want to take the easy way out. Often, this means ignoring the problem and leaving it for the next administration or proposing privatization for parts of the infrastructure. The United States, through Federal, State and local governments, spends about 2.4 percent of GDP (Gross Domestic Product) on infrastructure per year, which is much less than many other developed countries.

China, on the other hand, spends about nine percent. In dollar terms, it spends more on infrastructure annually than North America and Western Europe combined. China, like many other nations such as Germany and Japan, looks to long-term goals. Meanwhile, the U.S. generally has shifted away from long-term goals to short-term fixes.

President Dwight D. Eisenhower understood that solid infrastructure is a military weapon. One of the major rationales he used in support of the interstate highway system was that it would facilitate the efficient movement of troops and military equipment across long distances.

Today, one of the easy political solutions to failing infrastructure is to propose privatizing large parts of it, most notably roads and bridges. Private companies alone are unable to finance the huge costs of these infrastructure projects, so they are granted massive tax breaks and are allowed to collect user fees such as tolls to offset their expenses.

This may work for some high-traffic spots in major metropolitan areas, but it will never work for rural roads and bridges that see relatively little traffic but are equally essential to the livelihood of the local population. The other issue is that the roads and bridges are still built with taxpayer money (in the form of grants and tax breaks), yet the taxpayers are charged tolls to use the very things they have already paid for.

Overall, transportation needs to be looked at more closely, and we need a variety of options so that if one part of the system breaks down, there is a backup. Currently, there is no backup, which is why one small failure in the highway system, for example, can cause weeks or months of disruption. Thus, a major blizzard has the potential to cripple cross-country rail networks.

'Houston, we have a problem'

The situation in Houston in the aftermath of Hurricane Harvey in 2017 was the "perfect storm" of infrastructure failures, environmental mismanagement and changing weather patterns. It was as much a man-made disaster as was Hurricane Katrina in New Orleans 12 years earlier.

One of the biggest issues in Houston was the lack of zoning and building codes, which are essential components for urban growth. Houston is the fourth-largest city in the U.S. in terms of population and the third-largest in area. More than 2.3 million people are spread out over more than 630 square miles.

Most cities have stringent building requirements. In San Francisco, which has a high population density because the city is confined to a small area, there are higher standards for buildings due to the threat of earthquakes. In addition, they don't build where there could be floods, and residential and business areas are strictly separated.

In Houston, much of the city was built in known floodplains. Houston was planned by developers, apparently with little thought given to how the various communities would deal with the inevitable floodwaters. Houston is a concrete jungle that floods regularly: The first major flood was in 1935, and since 1994 it has flooded several times. There was a 100-year flood in 1994, a 500-year flood in 2001, and devastating floods in 2015, 2016 and 2017.

The 2017 flood was the worst, of course. With so much of the land paved over, with so many lawns unable to absorb more than an inch or so of rain and with Hurricane Harvey being bigger and slower than previous storms, there was simply nowhere for the water to go.

To make matters worse, the lack of building regulations meant that not only were thousands of homes built in floodplains, but when there was a plan to deal with excess rainwater it often involved simply moving that water to the next community via pipes, ditches, and so on. This total lack of infrastructure planning made the environmental disaster worse than it should have been – and completely predictable.

* * *

It's not just Houston, of course, although we know that many of the problems faced by Houston could have been averted or lessened with sensible and proper planning.

Just weeks after Harvey hit Texas, Hurricane Maria slammed into Puerto Rico, severely damaging the island's fragile infrastructure and knocking out power to almost the entire population of about 3.5 million people.

Instead of doing all in his power, as quickly as possible, to help millions of American citizens who were without electricity and were running dangerously low of drinking water and food, President Trump belittled the island's elected officials, calling them "politically motivated ingrates" who "want everything done for them."

The inadequate Federal response in Puerto Rico was all too familiar. I had seen it before in 2005 in New Orleans – and here we were a dozen years later and we were still stuck on stupid.

Overall, we're facing a national crisis that could affect 60 million people in low-lying and coastal areas. As a nation, we have no plan to protect those people. There is no Federal agency for planning a response. And the Trump administration is making matters worse by denying there is a problem, refusing to accept the scientific evidence.

* * *

One way to be better prepared for future hurricanes is to enlist the aid of the U.S. military – a "Ready Brigade," a quick-response Task Force that could move in immediately after the storm has passed.

This Task Force would be made up of Army, Navy and/or Marines. It could be drawn from the Army's 82nd Airborne Division, or the 101st Airborne Division, or the 10th Mountain Division.

The first of the military personnel could be on the ground in a matter of hours, assessing the damage, saving lives, helping people in distress. Such an operation would involve perhaps 15 to 20 ships, 100 helicopters, and a brigade of soldiers, including some who would parachute into the heart of the affected area.

I think Congress should authorize the funding in the Defense Department budget that would enable such a Task Force to be our nation's first responders for disasters involving hurricanes of Category 3 strength or higher.

Now, the Task Force wouldn't take the place of the various State National Guards and other first responder groups that have been at it for decades. It would supplement what's already being done, and it would do so with extraordinary speed, the likes of which the world has never seen!

* * *

It would be easy to slip backwards into being a third world country. We planned our metropolitan areas to be densely populated, but we haven't put enough thought into how to support that population in times of crisis.

How do they evacuate?

How do they survive if the railroads fail or if the electricity supply fails?

How do they deal with floodwaters?

Hurricane Katrina in New Orleans in 2005 was a learning experience. Mistakes were made, but there was no precedent. Katrina became the precedent and was the starting point for how to deal with future disasters. Houston, Florida, and Puerto Rico incorporated some of the lessons, but neglected others.

* * *

The compromised infrastructure across the United States is a serious threat to national security, and it's made worse by changing weather patterns and cities springing up where they perhaps don't belong.

We have vested interests in keeping the status quo, but the status quo is rarely favorable to the population at large. Human nature never changes, and those with power don't want to relinquish it. Unless we learn from history, we are doomed to repeat it – and the failure to learn from Hurricane Katrina is already having serious implication for our ability to deal with today's monster storms.

What we have to understand is that the price tag to keep Americans safe isn't the main issue. Look at the amount of money we spend on overseas wars and defense contracts. If we spent just a fraction of that on being prepared for disasters at home, we would be better able to take care of our own people.

The fact that we are failing in our duty to protect our own people is not just stupid, it's shameful and grossly negligent – but completely reversible if we can muster up the will to address these issues.

——— *Calls to action* ———

1. Accept the reality of changing weather patterns, and plan accordingly.

2. Build sustainable houses and rebuild in safe places, not in floodplains.

3. Don't use chemicals on your lawns.

4. Help trees work with the environment, not against it.

5. Devote time and effort to building a strong infrastructure.

6. Don't keep making the same mistakes ... don't get stuck on stupid!

Chapter 5

Guns 'n' stupidity

Talk sense to a fool and he calls you foolish.

- Euripides

The week after Martin Luther King Jr. was killed, in early April 1968, I ran into one of my cousins.

He was worried about my safety, because I was driving often between my home, in Lakeland, Louisiana, and Southern University in Baton Rouge. And at that time there was a lot of civil unrest in Baton Rouge and elsewhere around the country. He asked me to take his old revolver with about six bullets in it, and I put it under the front seat of my black and white '57 Chevrolet Bel Air. That was a real cool car with a hard top and black seats.

A few nights later, I was driving home when I saw

this old white guy trying to bum a ride, so I stopped to pick him up. He was dressed well, but his clothes were worn out. He had a business coat on, his hat was kind of cramped up, and he wore the remnants of a tie. Poor guy, he just looked like he got lost in the woods one day and never made it back home.

We started talking, and I told him I was attending Southern and was in ROTC. He told me he used to be a successful businessman with a nice family and a car and everything, but alcohol and drugs basically ruined his life.

"Let me ask you something," he said, very much aware of the racial tensions in the South at that time. "What gave you the courage to pick me up?"

"You looked like you were a long way from home, and besides, I wasn't worried," I said.

"What do you mean you're not worried?" he asked.

"Because I'm packing heat," I said.

He shook his head and was silent for a minute. After a while, he put his hand on the dashboard and turned to me.

"Can I give you a piece of advice? You seem like a nice young fella," he said.

He paused.

"As soon as you can, get rid of that gun. It makes you feel like you're 10 feet tall, doesn't it? Makes you feel invincible?"

"Yes, sir," I said. "I'm not scared of nothing with this thing sitting right here."

I didn't tell him that I hadn't figured out whether the thing would even shoot, but the very concept of having it within arm's reach emboldened me to pick up a scraggly guy I'd never met before on a dark road.

When I dropped him off, he thanked me.

"Remember what I told you. Get rid of that damn gun, because it's going to give you the courage not to walk away," he advised.

Those words struck home, and I can tell you right now that if you were to take the road to the church where I was baptized, and you go about a half mile to Bayou Chenal, and you stay on the right hand side, about eight feet off the bridge you'll find that revolver in the bayou.

In that moment, on that night, I learned a life lesson, and I learned it from a drunk!

Our culture is obsessed with guns

In my family, guns were used for hunting and gathering. We slaughtered our own meat and hunted in the lean winter months for deer and rabbit and other things to eat. We also shot at cans or bottles for sport and sometimes even shot at critters in the bayou.

From that, we learned a great respect for what guns can do.

I still own an old single-barrel goose gun I acquired in high school. It looks like something from the Civil War, but it was what poor people used for hunting. I also inherited the rifle my Dad used for killing pigs and hunting squirrels.

When I was in the Army, I couldn't go hunting with the guys because I didn't have a gun, so I bought a Champion shotgun from a sergeant for $60. I've still got that gun today.

As a general officer in the Army, you can buy the 9mm pistol you were issued, so I bought that gun for about $500. My non-commissioned officers also gave me a .44 magnum long barrel when I retired.

Another gun I own I got when I was chairman of the Louisiana Bicentennial Commission in 2012. We were raising money for the bicentennial, so we decided to produce a nice .12-gauge Browning shotgun with a commemorative engraving that we sold for $1,812 to honor the year (1812) that Louisiana became a state. This wasn't an urban cowboy gun; it was one you could go hunting with. And they gave me the first gun in the series.

This may sound surprising from someone who spent 37 years in the Army, but even though I've got all these guns at home, I refuse to carry one in my truck. In fact, the last time I had a gun in my vehicle was when I drove to Bayou Chenal to get rid of that revolver.

* * *

Guns are a part of our culture, but somewhere along the way over the last 200 years we made a conscious shift away from guns being primarily for hunting and protection.

Culturally, this shift was influenced by the cowboy tradition as we knew it through movies and television shows. We glamorized the power of the pistol and the rifle in shows like *The Lone Ranger*, *Bonanza*, *The Big Valley* and *Gunsmoke*, where the good guy with a great-looking horse would shoot people every now and then.

In the movies, we had everyone from John Wayne to Dirty Harry using guns to clean up America. Guns slipped into our culture as a way to solve problems.

What's more, guns have remained a mainstay of television shows, and in 1998 the American Psychiatric Association estimated that by the time he or she reached the age of 18, the average American child had seen 16,000 simulated murders and 200,000 acts of violence.

Since then, with unlimited access to the Internet and the profusion of violent video games, it wouldn't surprise me if those numbers have doubled or tripled.

Shooting people and blowing up things has become normal, which is kind of scary because it reinforces the notion that we can carry a gun anywhere – and that anyone who stops us is violating our Constitutional rights.

*   *   *

As a career soldier and a student of history, I

understand the history of our country and that our ancestors won our freedom through sometimes-violent encounters. Without guns in the hands of our ancestors, we would not be free today.

Hunting and home defense developed into a badge of freedom for our nation, because unlike ordinary citizens in other countries, we had the freedom to protect our homes and to go out and find our own food without asking for anyone's permission. Out of this grew the concept of the right to bear arms.

Today, there are more guns than people in America – as many as 350 million guns. The United States leads all nations in gun ownership. The next country is Yemen, a lawless state overrun with terrorists, with about one gun for every two people.

These numbers are disturbing, but the rate of gun ownership is decreasing. Up to 78 percent of Americans don't own a single gun. This means that less than one-quarter of the population owns all the guns – and that includes folks like me who are collectors and hunters.

However, only three percent of Americans own 50 percent of the guns. The average person in the top three percent owns about 17 guns.

What's frightening is that somewhere along the line, we as a nation created this attitude that anybody can have a gun at any time and in any place. It's almost like a birthright. For a segment of our population, guns are no longer for hunting or defending our home. They have become a political tool that

A lesson from London: Why do we ignore gun violence?

On March 22, 2017, an attacker armed with a knife killed four people, including a police officer, in London, England. In this age of 24 hour per day news, the story dominated every TV news channel and the front page of many newspapers.

On the very same day, 41 people were shot and killed across the United States, including four in Rothschild, Wisconsin, and three in Crowley, Louisiana.

Not to diminish the tragedy of what happened in London, but why does the world stop and watch when four people are killed in London – but nobody seems to pay attention to the fact that we are killing dozens of our own people every single day? Gun violence is so common in our own communities that it barely makes the news anymore.

Imagine, however, if just one of those dozens of people was killed by a terrorist. We'd have seen many days of round-the-clock reports covering every angle of the story. Terrorism is a real threat, but since 9/11 an average of just one American per year has been killed on U.S. soil by foreign-born terrorists. Think about it.

too often drives the debate about freedom.

I've been to England, and they don't have this problem. The police don't carry guns except in extraordinary situations, but they do carry batons, which they use to maintain order in an environment where nobody is carrying a gun.

I've been to France, and they don't have this problem. I've been to Spain, Norway, Egypt, Kuwait, pre-war Iraq, Jordan, Bangladesh, Pakistan, India and dozens of other places, and they don't have this problem.

This is something peculiar to our culture – more specifically, the gun industry's voice that has been relayed through the lobbyists and that has been allowed to inordinately influence our culture. Gun sales reached a record high of more than 5.5 million in the year after Barack Obama's election as President in 2008; sales nearly doubled in the year after his re-election in 2012 to about 11 million. It's no wonder Obama has been called the world's best gun salesman!

The National Rifle Association (NRA) has as many as five million members, so they're a powerful lobbying group, and they played on people's fears that Obama would try to implement some gun-control measures. The major thing Obama tried to do was to bring in some modest background checks after horrific massacres, such as the Sandy Hook Elementary School shooting in Connecticut in 2012 in which 20 children and six adult staff members were killed.

Even though the number of guns increased dramatically in the Obama years, the rate of gun ownership did not increase. In other words, the people buying these guns were already gun owners.

In 2016, when it appeared that Hillary Clinton might win the Presidency, Americans bought a record 27 million guns. They were motivated by fear – stoked by politicians and the NRA's lobbyists – that Clinton would take people's guns away and impose gun controls. By contrast, gun sales plummeted when Donald Trump won the election.

Carrying a gun is a great burden

America is in denial that we have a gun problem.

In 2016, more than 15,000 people were killed by gun violence in the United States, and another 30,000 were injured. That means we are killing more than 40 of our own people every single day; we are killing and maiming 10 children every day.

Gun violence also includes suicides, which account for another 21,000 or more deaths each year. In total, we're losing about 100 people a day – including about 20 military veterans – to gun violence.

To put this in context, we lose as many people in the United States to gun violence in a typical 2-year period as we lost in the entire Vietnam War. Imagine putting up a Vietnam Veterans Memorial every two years for the victims of gun violence.

Just across the border in Canada, there is less than

one gun death per day. In the United Kingdom, there is less than one gun death per week.

In America, every community is affected by guns. No city, no county and no state is spared from the horrible impact of gun violence.

In fact, firearms are one of the top five causes of death in the United States for people under 65. Under normal circumstances, this would be a major public health crisis, but the Centers for Disease Control and Prevention – the public health agency of the United States – is prohibited by a 1997 law from conducting any research that might "advocate or promote gun control."

Those who represent the gun industry want us to believe guns are not the problem. They say, "Guns don't kill people, people kill people." They have taken the legitimate right to bear arms and totally confused it with the right to carry a weapon anywhere.

What the lobbyists advocate is not practical and not always logical. For instance, you cannot carry a weapon into an NFL stadium or a concert in an arena. When you have that many people packed together, many drinking alcohol in an emotionally charged situation, there's a good reason you cannot take a weapon in there.

However, people can take a weapon into the grocery store and stroll through the park in the middle of the day with a gun to exercise their own loose interpretation of the right to bear arms. These are generally accepted by the public as safe places to take children, but they're being turned into potential war zones.

In many states, you can carry a firearm into a bar, into a church, onto a college campus, and in almost any public space. In Atlanta, you can carry a gun on the MARTA mass transportation commuter trains, but the MARTA police are prohibited from carrying firearms. Even more absurd, having a mental illness is often not cause enough to prevent a person from owning a gun and carrying it in public.

As a result, we've got mentally ill people out there with guns who just start shooting – people like John Russell Houser in Lafayette, Louisiana, and James Holmes in Aurora, Colorado, who opened fire in movie theaters. Before they reached that point, both shooters raised multiple red flags about their mental stability, but nobody seemed to know the protocol for dealing with the situation.

The dilemma with a mentally unstable person is that we have to find a reasonable balance between the right to privacy and keeping the public informed that this person may be carrying a loaded gun in public.

* * *

If you're carrying a firearm, what is your vision for carrying it?

I have a vision when I take my gun into the woods. My vision is that this big deer will come up and present himself.

When you walk around with that gun in town, you are looking for who you think may want to harm you. Instead of walking away, you might decide to "stand your ground" and start shooting.

In 2014, this is exactly what happened in a movie theater in Tampa, Florida. Retired police officer Curtis Reeves got into an argument with Chad Oulson because Oulson was using his cell phone in the theater. Oulson threw a bag of popcorn at Reeves, and Reeves responded by shooting and killing him.

Taking a gun into the movie theater was like begging for trouble. The shooter was emboldened by having his gun. After the incident, he tried to use Florida's notorious "stand your ground" law as a defense. The gun and the law gave him the courage to do something he probably would not have done otherwise. That's about as stupid as you can get!

In fact, Reeves knew immediately he'd made a mistake.

"As soon as I pulled the trigger, I said, 'Oh, shoot, that was stupid,'" he told detectives shortly after the shooting. "If I had to do it over again, it would have never happened. But you don't get do-overs."

*   *   *

You've got to be mentally prepared to fire a gun. I spent years patrolling in South Korea and working with my troops during Desert Storm, and we constantly visualized what we might see and how we might need to react to a situation in which we needed to fire our guns.

In the 1980s, I was stationed in Germany when the anarchist group Red Army Faction tried to blow up our Army headquarters in Heidelberg, and the paramilitary Red Brigades kidnapped Brigadier General James L. Dozier. The Army increased security for all of our generals, and since I was *aide-de-camp* to Major General Neil Creighton, I carried a pistol everywhere I went for about a year.

That was the biggest burden I ever had in my life. Every time we went off the base, I was in uniform. I was never off duty, and that gun never left my side. This was the Cold War era, and there was nowhere safe to leave my gun. I couldn't even get a beer with the guys, because I couldn't be carrying a gun and drinking.

I never drew my pistol, but I was always scanning the scene. When you have that weapon, you are always visualizing.

That's why the idea of open-carry scares the hell out of me. It changes the dynamics for the police officers, too, because when they come to a scene and everyone has a gun, how do the cops determine the "good guy" with a gun from the "bad guy" with a gun?

These days, it's not uncommon to see a guy carrying a pistol around a shopping mall. Not a cop, just an ordinary guy. Why does he need to open-carry at the mall? What sense does that make? I can only imagine that someone carrying a weapon in the mall must be looking for potential targets. Could I be one? What does he perceive his potential threat to be?

If I see a dude with a gun, I go the other way. Who knows who is going to piss him off or get into an argument with him? If he's packing heat, he's looking for trouble.

Like that old guy told me in the car all those years ago, if you've got a gun, you tend to want to stand your ground instead of walking away. You've got that false sense of courage.

* * *

The right to bear arms means that I can have a gun in my house, and the law says I can have one in my car because it's an extension of my home. But this idea of carrying a gun to the mall or the grocery store is a new way of thinking that your home extends to the space around you wherever you go.

What most people don't realize is that it's a burden to carry a gun, and there are many responsibilities that go with it.

I commanded the 2nd Infantry Division in South Korea, which is one of the most dangerous regions in the world. I commanded troops in Saudi Arabia during Desert Storm. I trained troops all over the world, and one of the things we did when we went back to the garrison, which is our sanctuary, is that we took all the guns and we locked them up because we had a responsibility to the communities where we lived to maintain control of those weapons.

Unless you're in a war zone, even the Army doesn't allow soldiers to bring their weapons into the mess hall or office buildings, because we don't want an accidental shooting. Before Desert Storm, a continuous safety problem was soldiers accidentally firing their weapons. These were troops trained in the use of firearms, so imagine the mayhem of untrained masses walking around with loaded guns.

In 2005, when I arrived in New Orleans as the military coordinator after Hurricane Katrina, I was shocked to find the troops and local police with their weapons trained on the local population as if they were the enemy.

"Get those damn weapons down!" I ordered. "Put the weapons down!"

We came to New Orleans to help our fellow citizens, and you can surely issue a lot more water and food if you're not pointing your weapon at somebody. We still had our weapons, but we didn't need to intimidate our own people.

Another decision I made was that our troops could not carry guns in establishments that served alcohol, because we had no way to secure our weapons. We were never off duty, and we should not be seen walking around with a beer in one hand and an M16 in the other. It wasn't going to happen on my watch!

Consequences of opposing
the pro-gun lobby

The debate over guns is divisive, to say the least.

Nobody could accuse me of being anti-Second Amendment, but I have lost speaking opportunities – and therefore income – because of my positions on guns, particularly on open-carry laws.

Others have taken a hit for similar positions, including U.S. Rep. Gabby Giffords of Arizona. In 2011, she was shot in the head in an assassination attempt in Tucson, Arizona. She survived but has brain damage, and six other people were killed and more than a dozen were injured. The weapon was a Glock pistol with a high-capacity magazine that allowed the shooter to get off 31 shots in a matter of seconds. He was stopped only when he tried to change magazines to continue the carnage.

Following her recovery from the attack, Giffords and her husband, astronaut Mark Kelly, started Americans for Responsible Solutions to try to control the gun industry. Among their aims are to limit the size of magazines, limit the definition of a sporting weapon, and control the sales of assault rifles.

They asked me to join them and I agreed. Now I'm a retired member of the Armed Forces that supports this idea of gun control. I'm not naïve, but I feel strongly that we have to speak about the unspeakable if we are going to make our world a better place.

Before they formed Americans for Responsible Solutions, Giffords and Kelly were national celebrities.

For about six months after they formed this organization, they were essentially blackballed, thanks to the efforts of people who were opposed to any limits on gun ownership. It wasn't until they became less vocal about gun control that they started to get back on track with speaking engagements and public appearances.

Mass shootings

Each year in the United States, there are about 360 mass shootings, or one nearly every day. A mass shooting is generally defined as an attack in which four or more people are killed or injured. Lately we've seen a steady progression of "the worst mass shooting in U.S. history": 32 people killed during a shooting spree at Virginia Tech in 2007, 49 people killed at a gay nightclub in Orlando in 2016, and 58 killed and more than 500 wounded in Las Vegas in 2017.

About 80 percent of mass shootings are committed by the legal owners of the weapons – a fact that is used by both sides of the gun-control issue.

For those who support gun control, this proves that guns are too easy to buy and that the current system of minimal background checks, if they're conducted at all, is ineffective. The opponents say it proves background checks don't work – which is true, but only because the checks are so weak.

Not all gun sales require background checks. In fact, only about three out of four people purchasing guns legally go through background checks, thanks

U.S. leads all nations in firearm death rate.
U.S. leads all nations in gun ownership.
(See the correlation?)

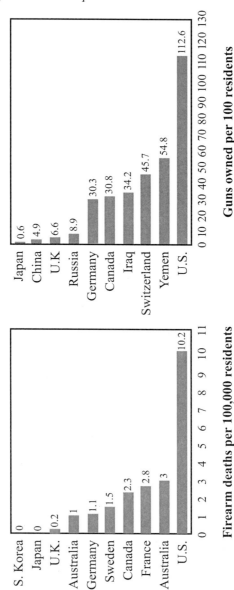

Firearm deaths per 100,000 residents

S. Korea	0
Japan	0
U.K.	0.2
Australia	1
Germany	1.1
Sweden	1.5
Canada	2.3
France	2.8
Australia	3
U.S.	10.2

Guns owned per 100 residents

Japan	0.6
China	4.9
U.K	6.6
Russia	8.9
Germany	30.3
Canada	30.8
Iraq	34.2
Switzerland	45.7
Yemen	54.8
U.S.	112.6

http://www.telegraph.co.uk/travel/maps-and-graphics/mapped-the-countries-with-the-most-guns/
http://www.amjmed.com/article/S0002-9343(15)01030-X/fulltext

to the so-called "gun show loophole" that requires checks only when you buy a gun from a federally licensed dealer.

The solution we are always offered to the epidemic of gun violence is to put more guns in the hands of more people and to loosen the open-carry laws. They want us to believe that the more guns you have, the more secure you are. That's total nonsense.

Studies have consistently shown that there is a direct correlation between more guns and more shootings that result in death and injury. This is true across all states, all age groups, and all income levels, regardless of whether the gun owners are male or female, urban or rural, or employed or unemployed. The greater the availability of guns, the greater the homicide rate.

On the other hand, states with stronger gun laws have less gun violence and fewer gun deaths.

* * *

Ever since 1981, when President Ronald Reagan was shot in an assassination attempt in Washington, D.C., any conversation about gun control or background checks is somehow interpreted as an attack on the Second Amendment. And every time the discussion comes up, more guns are sold.

The gun-control measures are never passed, but we've got to remember that there is a whole industry dependent on keeping doubt and fear in the public's mind.

Polls consistently show support for background checks at 90 percent or more, including among gun owners. More than 75 percent of people support a license requirement to purchase a gun. A majority of people believe buying guns is too easy and that they would be less safe if more people carried guns.

Only 14 states require a permit to purchase a firearm or a license to own a firearm. But Iowa, Maryland, Michigan, Nebraska, New York, North Carolina and Rhode Island require a permit or license only for handguns.

Many people who use guns to commit violent acts, including murder, not only had access to guns but under the current rules they had a right to bear these arms. This is just stupid, and the politicians who refuse to take action have to bear some of the responsibility.

The things we need to keep in mind are that the majority of Americans do not own guns and the majority also want some control over who can own guns and where they can take their guns. Yet we've allowed the minority to dominate the debate and tell the majority what to do.

We've got to stop being stupid and distracted from the real problem of gun violence. We've got to start making informed decisions about the real threats to our society – starting with the guns that are taking the lives of so many in our communities.

Among the high-profile gun-related crimes committed in the U.S. are assassination attempts on Presidents and candidates for public office. **Above:** *President Ronald Reagan waves to bystanders outside a Washington, D.C., hotel a moment before being shot by John Hinckley Jr. on March 30, 1981.* **Below:** *Secret Service agents attend to two of the people who were struck by bullets during the Reagan assassination attempt.*

———— *Calls to action* ————

1. Avoid people who are carrying guns, unless they are trained law-enforcement or military personnel.

2. Have the courage to walk away from potentially violent situations.

3. Don't carry a gun in public.

4. If you own a gun, keep it under lock and key when you're not using it.

5. Don't use guns to resolve problems when making movies and TV shows.

6. Don't keep making the same mistakes; don't get stuck on stupid!

Chapter 6

Educational system in need of repairs

Nothing in all the world is more dangerous than sincere ignorance and conscientious stupidity.

– Martin Luther King Jr.

My dad was a hard-working farmer who never learned to read. He could recognize road signs and pictures and numbers, so he knew he was on Hwy. 90, for example, but someone else would have to fill in the blanks for him.

I was the eighth of 12 kids and the first in my family to go to college.

One of the warnings that teachers used to give us was that if you don't know how to read, you're not going to be able to write a check. You won't be able to read a newspaper. And if you like sports, you won't be able to read the sports pages.

It was a success-or-failure situation if you didn't

Under-funding of public education chips away at the cornerstone of American society and ultimately weakens our democracy.

know how to read. Maybe you weren't the brightest student and couldn't do algebra, but that's stuff you might get later. If you couldn't read, you'd never understand algebra.

In the 19th century, the promise of education was key to the U.S. becoming a world superpower, but not every group of people had a fair chance at a good education. All across the country, even into the mid-20th century, the schools were racially segregated, and in many cases there were no high schools for minority students until after World War II.

When I was growing up in Lakeland, Louisiana,

there was a high school about a mile from our house, but I had to catch a school bus at 6:15 a.m. and ride for an hour and 15 minutes every morning to Rosenwald High School in New Roads – then take the bus back every afternoon. Rosenwald had been established for black students after World War II. Three of my older brothers didn't go to high school at all – because the only school they could have attended was in Baton Rouge, 26 miles away, and there was no way to get there.

Although everyone knew that wasn't fair, it was agreed on that everybody had a chance to go from the cotton field to the board room – but only if you had an education.

That expectation is still alive today, but the reality of this concept is constantly being challenged.

Education is the key
to climbing out of poverty

Education is one of the universal expectations of our democracy. It was and is part of the deal – the belief that education is crucial, not only to building our economy but to having functional, literate people.

Since its early days, our democracy has included a tax base for important public services such as law-enforcement, sanitation and education. Among other things, we had to teach our children to read. Instead of having each one of us do it, we decided to have an educational system.

Collectively, we bought in to a form of self-governance:

We elect our officials and we pay taxes so we can get common services that provide us a safe community, safe water, sanitation and education for our children.

As the United States became less rural and more urban, technology and other things changed, but the basic premise of how we fund public education has not changed in terms of it being a tax-based system.

Over time, however, we've created a convoluted educational system that doesn't make a lot of sense. It's overwhelmingly stupid! We've got public schools, private schools, parochial schools, charter schools, magnet schools, home schools and who knows what else. This is stupid, because it disperses public and private money in so many different directions. It may benefit individual kids or groups of kids, but it hasn't done much to improve our educational system as a whole.

Are we really better off with more varieties of education?

There is something essentially wrong with what we've done in education over the past couple centuries. I don't think it's intentional, but things have gotten out of whack at the federal, state and local levels.

*   *   *

A glaring example of how good intentions can go awry is Warren Easton High School, a charter school in New Orleans. It was the first school that opened after Hurricane Katrina, which devastated New Orleans in 2005, and it is now part of the first all-charter school district in the nation. I've gone there many times, including once with former President George W. Bush, 10 years after Katrina. We were visiting the Laura Bush Library – named for the First Lady, because she raised a lot of money for it. The Louisiana Superintendent of Education, New Orleans Mayor Mitch Landrieu and other dignitaries were also there.

People were telling us about the success of the charter program in New Orleans. They talked about the improvements being made in the school systems and the 90 percent graduation rate, but clearly some problems were not being addressed.

They were about to move on when I spoke up:

"Wait! Hold it! Mr. President, may I make a comment?"

President Bush knew I could be opinionated, so he joked that he didn't want to hear what I had to say. I said it anyway.

"Here's what we've got to speak about, Mr. President."

I told them that Tulane University had recently published a paper saying there were 14,000 students in New Orleans who were on the streets and not going to school. I also told them that charter schools normally have a rigid policy on who they accept. Unlike the public schools, they don't have to take everyone who shows up at their door.

If you have a kid who talks a little slow, you don't have to accept him – and there is no accountability for that decision. Within the first few weeks of school, if Little Johnny is acting up, you can expel him without being accountable to anyone.

"So, I'm asking you this: Is that right or wrong?"

My point was to challenge the practice of a school not having to be accountable for the students under its control. Each charter school has its own school board, and it's even worse when we the taxpayers are footing the bill but apparently have no right to know anything other than what the charter school corporations want us to know.

The school representatives tried to explain their way around what I was saying, but everyone knew I was telling the truth. When you get to select the students and you can dismiss them without any accountability, you damn well ought to have a 90 percent high school graduation rate – because you've eliminated the kids who are behind and have problems. These are the kids who end up in the public schools or out in the streets.

* * *

If you go to where our worst public schools are in Louisiana – places like St. Helena or Pointe Coupee parishes – you will find a very poor property tax base. At the other end of the spectrum, if you go to the more affluent communities with higher tax bases like St. Tammany and St. Charles parishes, their schools are consistently at the top of the public schools rating system.

In some of the richest school districts, every kid gets an iPad or other computer, which he or she can take home to help with homework. These kids automatically have an advantage over kids in the lower third of the population who go to schools with poor infrastructure and who don't have resources like broadband Internet.

In Louisiana, we could have had broadband Internet in every school a number of years ago, but then-Governor Bobby Jindal said "no," because the program would have been funded with Federal money – in direct competition with private businesses. He was in a perpetual campaign for President, and he thought taking Federal money would alienate him from his Republican base, who disapproved of the Federal control that comes with Federal funds.

* * *

In many poor Louisiana communities, about 80 percent of the property is owned by 20 percent of the people – and the 20 percent don't send their kids to public schools. They go to parochial or private schools.

And even though the 20 percent are not the majority of voters, they control the system in those communities. They are prominent in politics and business, and they have been successful in keeping property taxes at a minimum.

As a result, there are poor public schools in those communities where they keep the tax base low. They can't fully support public services like water and schools, and they continue to erode the basic principle that the purpose of government is to serve the public at large as opposed to serving business.

That's stupid, and it perpetuates the problem, because without a decent education it is almost impossible for poor kids to climb out of poverty.

The new normal: economic segregation in schools

There are two areas where government seems to think that private businesses can solve America's problems. One is education and the other is prisons. What they've done in education is that they created an economic model where charter schools in particular – unlike the public schools – aren't required to carry the burden of teacher healthcare or retirement programs.

Many of the charter school teachers are brand new college graduates or are retired public school teachers. The retired teachers are drawing two checks (one of which is from their retirement plan), and they already have health insurance. The new teachers are young and healthy, so it may not matter to them that benefits like health insurance and retirement pay aren't part of the deal, or they may feel that they don't have an option in today's workforce.

The result is that these schools can employ teachers

for less money than the public schools can, but the per-student cost to the taxpayer is about the same. The average teacher in a charter school is paid about $44,000, while a public school teacher makes an average of about $53,000. The difference frequently goes to the bottom line as a corporate profit instead of being reinvested in better schools and higher pay for teachers.

At one point in time when I was growing up, California had the best schools in the world, then some contrarian came up with Proposition 13. He asked:

"Why am I paying such high taxes on *my* property so *your* kids can go to school?"

The simple answer to that question was best expressed by the writer John Green:

"It's because I don't like living in a country with a bunch of stupid people."

Nonetheless, in 1978 California voters passed Proposition 13, basically limiting property taxes and, as a result, restricting the level of funding that goes to the school system. The result: California's school system ranks in the bottom fourth of all states.

* * *

The challenge we get into is that vouchers and charter schools further divide taxpayer money and other resources that should be going to the public schools. In Baton Rouge, Louisiana, it is so upside-down. The public school buses pick up the public school kids early in the morning and take them to a transfer point someplace. Then, the buses go to pick up the private school kids.

That's how stupid it is. Public money for private schools!

What's more, we need to challenge ourselves on the question of whether we have taken a step backward toward segregation. We've gone full circle from "separate but equal" school systems to integration and now to economic segregation – where the rich kids go to good schools with good resources and the poor kids go to poor schools with poor resources. This is happening all over the country, even in places like New York, where generally there are good schools and good school systems.

Are we really better off now with the new system?

Today, we've got vouchers, charters and magnets, and we can't always tell which is which. I once spoke at a school that I thought was a public school. The principal invited me to speak because one of the students had committed suicide, and I agreed to give them a motivational speech for free. As it turns out, it was a charter school run by a corporation with plenty of money.

The corporation also ran several other schools, and their primary purpose seemed to be to make money. I got so angry, I told them I was a *public* speaker and they hadn't told me they were a *private* company. I felt like they had misled me.

The principal at this school was the fourth in six years. He was hired by the corporation, not the public school board, so he wasn't accountable to anyone except the corporation and its shareholders.

By contrast, I had two principals in my entire life, one in elementary school and one in high school. They were entrenched in the community and they clearly wanted the best for the kids. I didn't see that kind of dedication in the principal at this charter school.

Corporations such as this one look at what we spend each year in taxpayer money per child – about $10,000 in Louisiana, $11,000 in Michigan and $7,500 in Arizona – and they ask, "What kind of profit margins can we make off it?"

It seems to me that too many charter schools are focused on profit margins and standardized test scores.

On a related note, "No Child Left Behind" is one of the policies that has not met its goals, either. Nowadays, teachers are "teaching to the test" rather than encouraging students to think for themselves. The schools have been conditioned to think all that matters is that the standardized test results come back okay.

The education disconnect: words vs. actions

There are clear discrepancies between what we *say* about education and what we *do*. When I spoke to the Louisiana School Boards Association's Southern Region Leadership Conference in 2016, Louisiana Governor John Bel Edwards spoke before I did, and he said the most important thing we do in a state is "educate our future," which is our children.

I'm sure Edwards had said the same thing dozens of times before, and every governor of every state would say the same thing, of course. It's a line that gets great applause every time, especially at a conference of educators.

But if it's true, why do we in America spend $10,000 a year to keep a child in school but $30,000 or more per year to keep a person in prison?

My state, Louisiana, is one of the biggest energy producers in the U.S., which means we should be bringing in tremendous amounts of revenue. Yet we're one of poorest states, the education budget is always being cut or in danger of being cut, and the state is always near the bottom in education scores.

If you want to know what's important to someone, look at where he spends his money.

Nationally, Louisiana is about average in terms of how much we spend per student per year: $10,000. States like New York, Connecticut, Massachusetts and New Jersey spend the most – anywhere from $14,000 to $20,000 per student.

In reality, that $10,000 we spend per student in Louisiana is an illusion. Due to a messed-up funding mechanism that's been in place for many years, a huge percentage of that $10,000 goes to the teachers' retirement fund, leaving much less for schools and teacher pay. In most other states, the retirement funding comes from a different source, meaning they spend the full amount on schools and teacher pay.

Can we honestly say that education is the most important thing when we consider the amount of resources we put into it?

* * *

Who's the most popular kid in high school? Is it the one who makes straight A's who's building a robot that one day might save lives, or is it the quarterback on the football team?

If you go to a college campus, same thing. Who's the most popular kid? Nearly all the students know the running back and the quarterback, but not the student who just got a half-million dollar grant to figure out how to produce clean water.

Or who gets paid more? There are probably several people in the Athletic Department who get paid more than the college president.

There's also a disparity with women in schools. Until I got to high school, all of my teachers were women. In fact, most of our schools are still run by women. About 85 percent of K-12 teachers are women (and that percentage keeps getting higher, up from 69 percent in 1969), more than half of all principals are women, and nearly half of the people who run the school boards are women. When I speak to school board associations and teachers' groups, it is no surprise to see that the audience is mostly women.

However, women have a disproportionately small influence in how our schools are run. Women tend to be the innovators in education, but – just as with corporate America – the system doesn't value or promote innovators. It promotes conformists, and the burden is put on women to go with the flow.

There is something fundamentally wrong or out of balance in terms of who is in charge of education. Women are often the best and the most motivated teachers, but they are dealing with a system that makes it hard to get ahead and make the changes that are necessary.

Another fact that many people find shocking is that women teachers are paid only about 90 percent as much as their male counterparts for the same work. Meanwhile, the real value of a teacher's salary – especially a female teacher's salary – has been in steady decline since 1960.

We say education is the most important thing, but we don't value teachers enough to pay them adequately to "educate our future."

We haven't made the system better, and that's what scares me. We continue to screw it up a little bit more each year. There are very few people who are generally happy with what's going on in education, except those who have their kids in good private schools and in states such as Virginia, Maryland and New York, which have great public schools.

We have friends who pay $20,000 a year for their kids to go to a private high school so they can get good enough grades to go to LSU and take advantage of the TOPS scholarship program. (TOPS – Taylor

Opportunity Program for Students – is a scholarship program in which private funds are matched by the State to cover a large portion of a college student's expenses.) The State-run program in Louisiana used to cover the tuition for about 50,000 students in State colleges and universities each year, but budget cuts in 2016 reduced the scholarship amounts from 100 percent to about 42 percent. Even with the cuts, many parents will still pay less for their kids to attend college than they paid for high school.

Once again, there is a disconnect between what we are told – that education is the most important thing the State government can do – and the reality that education is consistently cut in favor of giving tax breaks to corporations and the wealthy.

That's stupid, and it doesn't bode well for the future.

It doesn't have to be that way, though. In Minnesota, they've proven that doing the opposite can be successful. Governor Mark Dayton increased taxes on the wealthy and invested heavily in education. Businesses responded favorably to an educated workforce, and now Minnesota has one of the healthiest economies in the nation.

The 'Uberization' of education

One of our problems in this country is that we are treating education like an entrepreneurial experience as opposed to a public service that is supposed to be provided equally to everybody. It's the Uberization of education, whereby schools and teaching are commodities that can be farmed out on demand, but with no expectation that the services will have a lasting impact. It's all about what's happening right now: Test scores and profits.

It's so stupid and convoluted, because instead of just building good schools inside poor neighborhoods, we give parents choices of different schools that bid on – or reject – their kids. The kids spend a chunk of the day on the bus or in a car going to a community that doesn't look like where they live.

My brother-in-law drives his grandson 15 miles to school in the morning, then somebody else has to get him at the end of the day. Some of the crazy traffic in America is the result of people taking their kids to school and back. We are creating traffic jams with this fleet of cars and buses moving kids all over the place.

In my neighborhood, guess what's passing by my house at 6:20 in the morning? A school bus. A big yellow school bus, taking kids to a bus transfer point.

In more than 60 years from the days when I caught the bus at 6:15 a.m., all we've gained is five minutes. And it's not just in my neighborhood. In New York, there are kids catching subways at that time in the morning.

There's something inherently wrong with this system. We've either over-engineered it to stupidity or we've under-engineered it to allow it to be stupid.

* * *

What worries me most about our educational system is the kids who drop out – those 14,000 or more who are not accounted for at all in New Orleans, for example. Those kids end up in the contraband economy. They are the ones who are shooting each other and will end up in prison.

Instead of working around the idea that education should be equal for everyone, we seem to be regressing.

The stupid part is that most of us have put the responsibility of education entirely in the hands of the schools. The school should be the assistant in the process of education. Parents must be in charge and they must be more involved, starting with the best leadership practices at home.

I often ask parents:

"When was the last time you had your child read a paragraph to you?"

"Do you go to all the PTA meetings?"

"Do you go to more sporting events than PTA meetings?"

As I explained in my book, *Leadership in the New Normal*, a family is a team, and getting your child to read to you keeps everyone engaged. The home-schoolers understand this, but the average family of two working parents has forgotten it. They are always going back and forth, picking up kids, dropping them off, going to soccer, going to tae-kwon-do, going to baseball and so on.

When you go to the PTA meetings, it shows you care about more than just sports and standardized tests.

The most important thing students can do is read, but they also need to learn how to observe and how to think. Not *what* to think but *how* to think. We have in some ways lost sight of the whole concept of how we educate and why we educate.

We have degraded education while at the same time pretending it's the most important thing we can do for our children.

That sounds to me a lot like being stuck on stupid. And we need to fix it before it's too late.

——— *Calls to action* ———

1. Teach every child to read.

2. Pay teachers more money.

3. Hold all schools accountable for every child and every dollar.

4. Restore the tax base to a level that sustains the schools more adequately.

5. Go to PTA meetings.

6. Don't keep making the same mistakes ... don't get stuck on stupid!

Chapter 7

Breaking the
cradle-to-prison pipeline

If stupidity got us into this mess,
then why can't it get us out?

– Will Rogers

ot long ago, I got a speeding ticket in
Florida, but I left it in the car and forgot
about it.

A couple months passed, so they sent me a reminder.
And while they were at it, they doubled the price of
the ticket because I didn't pay it in the first 30 days.

I also got a parking ticket in New Orleans when
the front part of my car encroached into a space
where only taxis are allowed to park. Ironically, I
was attending a volunteer meeting to help the city. I
forgot about the ticket, and the police said if I didn't
pay they were going to put a warrant out for me. This
$30 ticket became a $90 ticket.

I had the money, so I paid these tickets and went on with my life. If you come from a middle-class family, it's just a bump in the road.

But what if you just don't have the means to pay?

If you don't pay your speeding tickets or parking tickets, you become a wanted person. About four out of every five defendants in the U.S. cannot afford a lawyer and must be appointed one by the State. But if you live in Louisiana, you probably won't get a public defender because there are only 300 to 400 public defenders when our state needs 1,700 or more.

Without the money to pay a lawyer or to pay the fine, you can end up in what amounts to debtor's prison.

Meanwhile, you can't work because you're in jail, so you can't support your family and you may lose your job. When you get out, you may be pressured into the contraband economy because, having a criminal record, almost no one will hire you.

Or take the case of a young man I know who spent seven years in prison for a minor drug offense, followed by two years on probation in a transitional job, during which time he was clean and became a supervisor. One day, he forgot to tell his probation officer about a quick trip to a neighboring state, where he got stopped for a minor traffic offense.

Because he left the state without permission, he was sent back to jail and lost his job.

We took someone who was a productive member of society and put him back into a regressive system

The notorious cradle-to-prison pipeline virtually pre-destines certain minority boys to a life behind bars. It may take a cultural shift, but more must be done to curb this shameful reality.

for no good reason.

Sure, the kid knew the rules and he chose to break them. But did the punishment fit the crime? It's almost like he was set up to fail.

The system is rigged against those without money or means, and that's unfair and plain stupid. Sending the poor to jail doesn't benefit anyone.

How the 'cradle-to-prison pipeline' keeps the poor in permanent fear

According to the Children's Defense Fund, a black boy born in 2001 has a one in three chance of going to prison in his lifetime, and there is a high correlation between a lack of reading skills and going to prison. This is a big part of what is known as the "cradle-to-prison pipeline" – and once you're in the pipeline, there are few escape routes.

In fact, if you are a minority boy and if you are not reading at the fourth grade level by the time you are 10 years old, you have a high probability of having a run-in with the police by the time you are 14 or 15.

Many people believe the absence of a parent – especially a father – or a male role model in the home is also a huge contributing factor.

This is a self-perpetuating cycle. If you come out of a poor urban community and the father goes to jail, there is a higher than average probability that somewhere along the line his children will be in the same situation. If a kid's mother or father is in jail, he's less likely to be interested in school, so he'll fall behind in reading skills.

The cradle-to-prison pipeline is so well understood that some cities and states reportedly study the reading levels of 10-year-old minority boys to determine how much prison space they will need in 10 or 20 years. It's practically a science, because they understand the connection between 10-year-old minority boys who can't read at the fourth grade level and the percentage who will end up in prison.

The kids become disengaged from school, and it's all downhill from there. About 85 percent of kids who enter the juvenile court system are functionally illiterate, and more than 70 percent of the prisoners in the United States can't read or they read below the fourth grade level.

I've visited quite a number of prisons and jails, and I know that a high percentage of prisoners are in there simply because they missed a court date, didn't pay a parking ticket or a ticket for a broken tail light, missed a child-support payment, or got drunk.

When a person is in jail, he has to wait until a

'*The cradle-to-prison pipeline is so well understood that some states study the reading levels of 10-year-old minority boys to determine how much prison space they will need in 10 or 20 years. It's practically a science. They understand the connection between these boys who can't read at the fourth grade level and the percentage who will end up in prison.* '

judge can see him – and since he can't show up for work, he's likely to lose his job and can't pay rent or buy food.

I fully understood the implications of the cradle-to-prison pipeline while I was volunteering at a relief shelter during the catastrophic floods of 2016 in south Louisiana.

A woman was in the shelter with her three children while her husband was out carousing. When he returned late at night, they got into an argument.

The security guard started to sort out the argument, but that sorry-ass husband says, "You know that wench has a warrant out." The police immediately ran her name, and it was true. She had a warrant for failing to show up for court for writing a bad check for $25, so the police arrested her.

To make matters worse, the State took control of

the children because the husband disappeared and left the children alone in the shelter. What did the children do to deserve this?

This is a cycle that happens to the poor. I felt sorry for that lady because she was trapped in a bad marriage and she was in jail because she wrote a bad check. Most of the rest of us would have paid the bank a fee and forgotten about it, but she had no money, thanks to her shiftless husband.

Those three children were already halfway into the pipeline, so the next morning I called the chief of police and told him I wanted to get this lady out of jail so she could be with her children. I drove down to the jail to get her out, gave her some money, and told her to get her children back.

This was an eye-opening experience for me, because it showed me how the cradle-to-prison pipeline works. We've got people serving time in jail for writing bad $25 checks. If you can't cover a $25 check, plus the penalties and fees that the bank piles on, how can you pay a court fee and an appearance fee and maybe a parole supervision fee?

And yet, we keep putting poor people in jail. That's the first step into the pipeline, and we've got to stop this cruel, stupid practice that grinds down the poor and vulnerable.

*   *   *

One of the ways we have attempted to provide

an escape route from the cradle-to-prison pipeline is through the Honoré Center for Undergraduate Student Achievement at Southern University in New Orleans. The Honoré Center assists African American males in college so they can serve as role models and teachers in urban settings. Even one black teacher in a poor black boy's life can decrease the risk of that boy dropping out of school by up to 40 percent.

The first night we took in Honoré Center men, we observed a young man who was quite emotional and teary-eyed. The administrator asked him what was wrong.

"This is the first time in my life I have a room to myself," he explained.

He and his siblings were being reared by their grandmother, because their mother was in jail and their father had been shot and killed on the streets of New Orleans.

His story touched me deeply. But in his case we have an opportunity to break the cradle-to-prison cycle by giving him a chance at an education and to be a role model for other at-risk youth.

The odds were against this student from the start, not only because he was a young black male, but because statistically the United States has the highest incarceration rate of any industrialized nation. Our country has only about five percent of the world's population, yet we have about 25 percent of the world's prison population. Furthermore, Louisiana

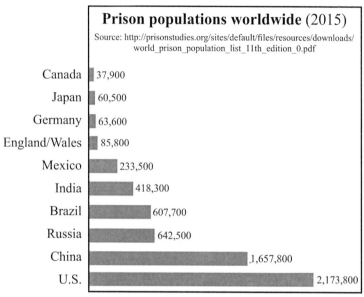

Prison populations worldwide (2015)

Source: http://prisonstudies.org/sites/default/files/resources/downloads/
world_prison_population_list_11th_edition_0.pdf

Canada — 37,900
Japan — 60,500
Germany — 63,600
England/Wales — 85,800
Mexico — 233,500
India — 418,300
Brazil — 607,700
Russia — 642,500
China — 1,657,800
U.S. — 2,173,800

In 2015, the U.S. had the highest rate of incarceration of any country in the world – nearly five times the world average. Its number of prisoners per 100,000 residents was 698, as compared with Canada's, for instance, which was 106.

has a higher incarceration rate than any other place in the world. It's no wonder Louisiana is known as "The World's Prison Capital."

This is a damn shame, but it doesn't have to be this way.

'Three strikes' has struck out

The number of people in jail and prison has quite an impact on other social programs. For example, believe it or not, some states spend more money on incarcerating their people than on educating them.

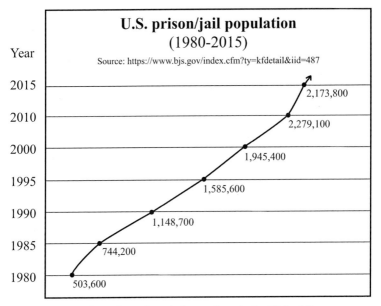

The number of people in jail or prison in the United States more than quadrupled between 1980 and 2015.

As a nation, we spend about $80 billion a year on prisons. It costs more than $30,000 per year to keep an inmate in prison, compared to about $10,000 to keep a student in school.

We definitely have an issue with stupidity when we are willing to spend three times more money on locking people up than on educating them.

We keep building more jails and prisons while we keep cutting the amount of money going to education.

I once asked a high-ranking politician in Louisiana

what we were going to do about our prison system and why so many of our citizens were being put behind bars. His answer:

"We have to build more prisons."

"No, no, no, no! That's not the solution!" I said.

When we put so many people in prison for minor offenses, that's "human capital" that is not contributing to the economy. And that's really stupid!

*   *   *

As long as we've had organized government, we've had jails to incarcerate people who behave badly. There are a lot of dangerous people who should be in prison for the safety of society. But nonviolent drug offenders make up more than 20 percent of the prison population, and there's no really good reason to keep them locked up at taxpayer expense.

The incarceration rate is exacerbated by "three strikes" laws, whereby three felony offenses – whatever they are – leads to a mandatory prison sentence of 25 years to life.

Look at what happened in California, an otherwise progressive state that introduced the three-strikes law in 1994. Now, they have a bunch of people in prison for life because they had three strikes against them for smoking pot. The stupidity is compounded by the fact that pot became legal in California in 2016, so they wouldn't be arrested for smoking it today.

Fortunately, in 2012, California's three-strikes

law was tempered by the passage of Proposition 36. One amendment to the law requires that the third offense must be a serious or violent felony for the offender to qualify for the stiffest sentence. Another amendment allows for the inmate currently serving a third-strike sentence to petition the court for a reduction of his term.

We have bought into a system where mass incarceration doesn't do anything other than take people off the streets. Prisons are called "correctional institutions," the connotation being that we are trying to correct something. People are punished because they did something wrong; so they get an opportunity to *correct* their behavior.

The problem is that the incarceration part works – but the correction part doesn't, because if you spend the rest of your life in prison, how can you show society that you've been *"corrected"*? As a result, people who are incarcerated can't take care of their children, and we produce another generation of young people who are being driven into the cradle-to-prison pipeline.

The problem with prisons is a complex subject, but we need to speak about the unspeakable and embrace a cultural shift. Every time we've had a cultural shift in America, it's happened because people were willing to speak up and speak about the unspeakable.

* * *

Right now, many people in power think things are just fine the way they are and it's just fine that we keep the prisons full. After all, it's a lucrative business for the growing private prison companies, which have guaranteed profits because they have guaranteed occupancy rates of between 80 and 100 percent. A lot of Wall Street guys have invested in these prisons, and they bank on State and local jurisdictions to keep them full in order to maximize profits. That's a hell of a set up!

We have incentivized the incarceration of our people, which is un-American, inhumane and the ultimate in stupidity. It also leads to corruption, as in the case of County Judge Mark Ciavarella Jr. in Pennsylvania, who was sentenced to 28 years in prison in the notorious "Kids for Cash" scandal.

Ciavarella was convicted of taking more than $1 million in bribes from developers of private juvenile detention centers, then presided over thousands of cases in which juveniles were sent to the detention centers for minor offenses. The more inmates these places had, the more money the detention centers made from the State. It is one of the most shocking examples of the corrupt system in which Americans' rights are trampled for the sake of someone else's greed.

Even if you get out of prison, the system can still be rigged and former prisoners can be exploited. Many states use something called "offender workforce development" that's supposed to be a way for prisoners to learn skills and get back into the workforce.

For $25 to $30 a day from the State, a business can take an ex-offender who's still on probation and put him to work for as little as 50 cents an hour. At the end of the month, the worker has only $100 if he's lucky.

It's cheaper for the State than keeping the person in jail, but it's impossible for the former inmate to get ahead on that sort of money. These are not dangerous people, so it's just another way to profit from the prison system and to turn human beings into profit centers. These ex-offenders would be more productive and would have a better chance at success if they were actually released and allowed to earn a living instead of being shackled to the State.

The reason the system stays in place is greed. Many employers want to keep a cheap source of labor, and we pretend we're doing the ex-prisoners a favor by teaching them workforce skills. In reality, this is only a step above slavery. In fact, there has been a theory in the African American community since the Reconstruction era that some states deliberately keep a large number of African Americans incarcerated. This way, they can take advantage of the free labor and virtually keep slavery alive.

* * *

When I was Commanding General in the First Army at Camp Shelby in Hattiesburg, Mississippi, we were training troops for Iraq and Afghanistan and we wanted to build a training facility that looked like an Iraqi village. Instead of putting out a contract to local businesses, I discovered the local sheriff would let us have all the carpenters and bricklayers we wanted through a company we called "Acorn Construction."

All of the workers in this company came out of the Mississippi criminal justice system. They were highly skilled people, and they built three villages for us at Camp Shelby. That was money we didn't have to spend, because it was practically free labor.

The prisoners were proud to make a contribution to the U.S. war effort in Iraq, but it bothered me to think how many of these people wouldn't have been in jail if they were properly represented in court or weren't being punished for being poor.

It was a waste of human capital, because those skilled workers should have been earning a living and taking care of their families. The stupid thing is, when we incarcerate people for petty crimes and their inability to pay fees, those people are not contributing to the economy. On the contrary, they're costing the economy.

If you get out on parole, many states – including Maryland, Texas and Louisiana – charge a so-called "parole supervision fee" that can range anywhere from $30 to $150 a month. The fee is a condition of parole, but it can be a severe financial burden and you can get sent back to jail if you don't pay it.

In a state like Maryland, the fee has nothing to

do with the ex-offender's court-mandated punishment. It is designed purely to subsidize the State's budget, which means the State is punishing those least able to pay.

One of the problems is that many judges have grown accustomed to giving maximum sentences for everything. Instead of using the maximum number of years as a guideline, they use it as a rule – and any judge who does otherwise is attacked for being "soft on crime." Their campaign slogan is, "I'm going to put these guys away," and they keep getting elected.

African Americans make up only about 13 percent of the U.S. population, but they are about 40 percent of the incarcerated population. To make matters worse, many of them shouldn't be there at all. Nearly half of all prisoners eventually exonerated of their crimes are African American.

The high price of free labor

In a strange way, the Louisiana State Penitentiary at Angola is setting an example of how prisons can help inmates reinvent themselves. The first time I visited Angola, it was a life-changing experience. This facility was once known as "The Bloodiest Prison in America," but the violence is minimal now because they put the prisoners to work and gave them a purpose. The prisoners contribute to their own well-being.

Many people know Angola for the famous rodeo where inmates not only ride the bulls but also man the concession stands and sell their handmade arts and crafts. It is one of the biggest events on the Louisiana social calendar.

At Angola, the inmates grow much of what they eat – vegetables, meat, crawfish, you name it – and they have one of best herds of cattle you will find in the entire country. They save the State a lot of money, and they even make money by shipping excess produce to other prisons. In the kitchen, the inmates are taught to cook.

Many of the prisoners learn new skills, and they take great pride in their work, whether they're serving food to visitors or picking okra in the field. The prisoners can also learn to read and take college-level classes. They can even earn a PhD while doing time.

All of this looks great until you realize that not many people ever come out of Angola alive. The average sentence for a prisoner in Angola is 90 years or more, and over 90 percent will never leave, even on parole. Think of all that human capital that could be fixing a car, building a house or working as a surgeon or college professor.

*   *   *

A lot of prisoners in America were caught up in the contraband economy or are victims of "three strikes" laws and are treated no differently than serial murderers.

Our challenge is how to find the right balance of

punishment for people who do not operate inside the norm of what we as a society have decided is acceptable behavior. In Louisiana, for example, you are going to jail if you get caught with marijuana, but in Colorado it's OK.

How stupid can we be? It's stupid to get picked up for such a petty offense as possession of a marijuana cigarette, and it's just as stupid to incarcerate someone for getting caught with one.

Early in the Donald Trump administration in 2017, the Attorney General of the United States decided to make things even worse. He vowed to crack down on non-violent drug offenses, even going so far as to claim that "good people don't smoke marijuana." His policies, if enacted, would be a windfall for private prison companies, which would be overflowing with new customers at great expense to the taxpayers.

In Louisiana alone, which incarcerates people at a higher rate than anywhere else in the world, a few simple changes to sentencing laws could save the State $300 million over 10 years and significantly reduce the prison population. Non-violent drug offenders, among others, could put their skills to work for the betterment of society instead of being thrown in prison and becoming a drain on taxpayer resources.

We've found a way to make money off prisons and prisoners, and now we have to find a way to keep more people contributing to the economy in a positive way and not send them to prison or jail for trivial offenses.

We need to find solutions, and the best solution is to address the issues at the source. Reading is the key, and in poor schools we should have two teachers in each classroom. It's worth it, because it improves the lives of the kids and it's cheaper than sending them to prison in 10 years. We also need worthwhile programs for the kids to participate in after school, such as a Boys and Girls Club or other volunteer organizations that help kids with their homework and keep them in school.

We can break the cradle-to-prison cycle if we want to. If we don't, we'll be trapped in stupidity forever.

—— *Calls to action* ——

1. Make sure all children can read.
2. Support an organization that helps kids with after-school activities.
3. Stop treating poverty as a crime.
4. Reduce sentences for minor offenses.
5. Get rid of "three strikes" laws.
6. Don't keep making the same mistakes ... don't get stuck on stupid!

Chapter 8

Healing the stupid in healthcare

There is no sin except stupidity.

– Oscar Wilde

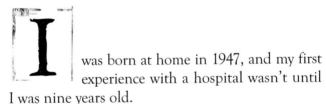was born at home in 1947, and my first experience with a hospital wasn't until I was nine years old.

My brothers and some other boys were playing baseball in the open field on the St. Alma School grounds on the plantation next to our farm in Lakeland, Louisiana. I was off to the side shooting marbles.

One my brothers swung the bat and it broke. The blunt end flew away and hit me in the head. There was a lot of blood, so they put me in the back of the farm truck to take me to the hospital. My Uncle Horace told my dad not to stop in Baton Rouge, which was about 25 miles away, but to keep driving to Charity Hospital in New Orleans.

Back then, Charity was segregated and nurses wore white uniforms. I woke up a day or two later, and this African American nurse held my hand and said, "Baby, how you doin'?" I saw the white hat and white stockings and white shoes, and I thought I must have died and gone to heaven. Then I saw my mom and aunt at the end of the bed, and I remember thinking, *This is kind of nice.*

That was public health at its best. You went to the hospital when you needed it, and you didn't worry about how much it would cost. I stayed in that hospital for about three weeks and they patched up my head, although the dent is still there today.

The other experience I had with the medical system when I was a youngster was when I was in elementary school and the doctors and nurses would come around to give us our mandatory immunizations. There was a real effort to make the public safe by controlling communicable diseases like polio and smallpox.

I grew up in a pretty efficient system, because it brought preventative healthcare to the people and recognized that not everybody had the means to get their children to the doctor's office for shots. It also showed that the community took pride in making sure every child was healthy, regardless of whether the family was rich or poor. If you were born unhealthy, though, the system didn't work for you.

Things have changed since I was young – and not always for the better. Medicine has become better and more advanced, but none of that matters if you can't get through the door to see a doctor.

Today, good healthcare is seen less and less as a human right or a community service and more as a luxury that is available primarily to those who can afford it.

As a result, we're hurting our own people – and we're stuck on stupid.

Greed is killing our healthcare system

With very few exceptions, most of us are just one cancer diagnosis or serious injury away from financial ruin. Even with new protections such as the Affordable Care Act – also known as Obamacare – which came into effect in 2010, the leading reason people go bankrupt in the United States is medical bills. Hundreds of thousands of personal bankruptcies each year are the result of medical bills, and as many as 64 million Americans struggle to pay these bills.

From cradle to grave, the healthcare system as we know it is one of our greatest challenges. If you can get through the door and find a good doctor and find a way to pay, it's almost like you are in dreamland. You can enjoy the ride and it can keep you alive for decades longer than our grandparents and great-grandparents could ever have imagined.

We have the best hospitals and the best medical clinics in the world, and most of them yield good

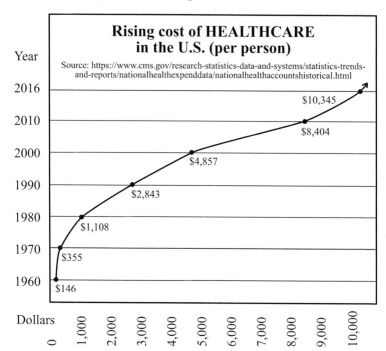

U.S. citizens spend more on healthcare than residents of any other country. Average healthcare costs are about $5,000 in Canada, $3,500 in the U.K. and $1,200 in Mexico. Average cost per person in the U.S. soared from $146 in 1960 to $4,850 in 2000 to $10,345 in 2016; in 56 years, that's a 70-fold increase.

results – but not everybody gets a ticket to dreamland.

The one thing that keeps millions of people out of the healthcare system is the cost. Whether you are poor, middle class or rich, the cost of healthcare is absolutely astronomical.

The price for a single aspirin that would cost less than 5¢ in a drug store can be $25 to $30 in a hospital, and a medical instrument that a surgeon can order online for $90 is billed through the hospital for $1,200. The cost of treating colon cancer is around $30,000 if it's caught early, hip replacement surgery costs an average of about $40,000, and treating a severe heart attack can cost up to $1 million.

Overall, the cost of healthcare tripled between 2001 and 2016, and the cost of healthcare for a typical American family of four was nearly $26,000 in 2016. Most of that can be covered by insurance or subsidies, but that same family still has considerable out-of-pocket expenses.

The cost of healthcare is projected to continue to increase by nearly six percent per year, which is at least triple the rate of inflation. This is not sustainable, and it's going to break the country. We just can't afford it. What's more, even though we spend more per person on healthcare than in any other advanced nation, people in many other countries live longer than we do.

* * *

Doctors and surgeons make good livings, but their salaries have not kept up with other professionals, so it's hard to put the blame on them. They are not the problem.

Some people might tell you that the runaway costs have to do with the cost of medical malpractice insurance. That might have been a respected argument at the turn of the 21st century, when people were suing over everything, but there are not as many lawsuits against doctors today as there used to be. The doctors and hospitals cleaned up their act, so you don't hear so many stories today about someone going into a hospital to have his left big toe worked on but coming out with his right arm missing. A big part of this is that doctors today rely more on computers and other technologies, so there's less risk of human error.

In fact, malpractice insurance for a typical family physician can be as low as $5,000 a year, which is less than most people pay for health insurance. The costs are actually going down, because the number of malpractice lawsuits has dropped significantly. Malpractice insurance is a contributing factor to high costs, but not a major one.

You can argue about whether the Affordable Care Act is good or bad, but either way it's an emotional argument. The creation of this program was a serious effort to open the door to healthcare for millions of people who had been left behind. It provides health insurance and healthcare for at least 20 million people, so the emotional attachment is real and raw. People who finally had health insurance and whose lives were saved do not want to go back to "the good old days" when it was too expensive to deal with health issues until it was too late.

It's no wonder the efforts to repeal the Affordable Care Act in 2017 were met with so much opposition.

Another contributing factor to rising healthcare costs is that the average newly minted doctor has nearly $170,000 in student debt from medical school.

That's crazy! It's like paying for an extra house. And a large number of doctors are still paying off their student debt 20 years later. We are all paying for that through increased costs to visit the doctor. Still, this element accounts for just a fraction of the huge increases in healthcare costs over the years.

The nub of the problem is that healthcare is a major industry that generates a lot of money and big profits. The number of new specialty clinics that have been built since 2002 is staggering. A lot of what these places provide is essential, but their services used to be provided by hospitals – and they all expect to make a good profit. Each clinic has the best equipment and its own operating rooms and its own staff, and none of that is cheap. For those of us who can afford it, these clinics can be lifesavers – but you don't get through the door unless your insurance pays for it or you can pay for it yourself.

* * *

One of the issues with the rising costs of the current healthcare system is that we as consumers are paying into a two-tier system. First, we're paying for insurance, which is an $850 billion industry that is enjoying healthy, record-breaking profits. Second, we're ensuring healthy profits for the healthcare providers – doctors, nurses, hospitals, etc.

This two-tier system is one of the major arguments for a single-payer system, because it cuts out the need for private insurance – and therefore saves a big chunk of money.

In addition, hospitals and clinics often charge higher fees if you have insurance than if you don't, because they know how much the insurance companies will pay. Of course, the insurance companies pass along those high costs to policyholders in the form of increased premiums, co-pays and deductibles.

Another issue is that we're being over-medicated. It is a commonly noted fact that the United States has only about five percent of the world's population but we consume more than 60 percent of the world's prescription drugs (including 80 percent of the world's prescription painkillers).

This, of course, is adding to the overall cost of our healthcare. The drug companies sometimes pressure doctors to prescribe more of the drugs they are selling – particularly the high-priced specialty drugs – and meanwhile the cost of those drugs keeps going up.

The average American spends more than $1,000 a year on prescription drugs, and more than half a million people spend that much every week. For the elderly, the average cost of prescription drugs is about $1,000 a month. Part of the cost is covered by private insurance or Medicare, but this is a huge contributing factor to the rising cost of insurance.

* * *

The end result is that healthcare is more expensive in the United States than in any other nation, and the only explanation left is greed. We have sold our healthcare to the highest bidders, and we stand around watching.

Many of us were raised with the understanding that hospitals were essentially nonprofit and their mission was to serve the public good. Yet, many so-called nonprofit hospitals – which make up about 60 percent of all hospitals – rake in huge profits. The top ten most profitable hospitals in 2013 each made more than $163 million in profit – and seven of the top ten are "nonprofits."

The University of Pennsylvania Medical Center in Philadelphia is also a nonprofit, and it made over $184 million profit in 2013. The CEO reportedly makes nearly $6 million a year, and at least 12 administrators make more than $1 million a year. Only a small percentage of its work is "charity." In a case like this, the "charitable" hospital does not serve the community in the same way that an institution like Charity Hospital in New Orleans once did.

In 2015, Martin Shkreli became the face of greed when he raised the price of the antiparasitic drug Daraprim overnight from $13.50 to $750.00 per pill. The drug was used to treat and prevent malaria, especially in sub-Saharan Africa and Asia, where more than a third of the population lives on about $1 a day. There are many other examples of high-priced drugs, but this was one that struck a chord with so many people because it was so extreme.

We know that we don't have to pay $40,000 for a hip replacement, because you can fly to India or Mexico and get it done for around $6,000. The quality is the same and the outcome is the same. You can go to Canada or Mexico and get the exact same drugs for a fraction of the cost you pay in the U.S. – because they don't jack up the price to the extent that we do in the U.S.

The costs don't have to be this high, but they remain high anyway – not for the good of the people but because of greed and to keep investors happy.

We also have to optimize technology to make the healthcare system more efficient and to keep the costs down. We need to have one database for all of our health-related records from cradle to grave – so we don't have to answer all the same questions everywhere we go and create new databases in every doctor's office and every clinic and hospital.

Increased efficiency also reduces the chance of misdiagnosis. Studies have shown that up to 30 percent of initial medical evaluations are wrong, a mistake that can be deadly but that can be corrected if doctors can see a patient's complete record.

The system's broken. But Congress is always trying to legislate healthcare matters and figure out how citizens can foot the bill – instead of keeping the costs down and treating healthcare as a human right.

That's infinitely stupid! Because if we have good

healthcare and treat people while they're healthy instead of when they get sick, we increase life expectancy, create a more productive workforce, decrease chronic diseases, and drive down overall costs.

Lifestyle changes are the key to good health

When I was growing up in Lakeland, we'd have boudin and cracklin' twice a year when we would personally kill a pig and have a *boucherie* on the farm. That stuff's not good for you, but it's okay once or twice a year. In south Louisiana today, you can buy boudin and cracklin' every day at every corner grocery store – but you can't eat that stuff every day and expect to stay out of the hospital.

It's the same with drinking alcohol, which was done mostly at social gatherings or just as an occasional indulgence – as opposed to coming home every evening and rewarding yourself with a few drinks after saving the world. That's a good way to develop cirrhosis of the liver!

This is something we *can* control. It's entirely our responsibility. In fact, for every finger we point to the failings of the healthcare system, we've got three fingers pointing back at us. One finger is telling us to eat better food, one tells us to quit smoking and use alcohol only in moderation (if at all), and the third is telling us to get out there and exercise.

Too many people are dying too young because of what they drink, what they eat and what they smoke – and because they're sitting on the couch watching

TV or playing video games instead of going outside.

The Amish have a very low cancer rate, which is attributable to their active lifestyle and the fact that they eat healthy food and don't smoke or drink, as a rule – and despite the fact that they have limited contact with doctors and the outside world. They live in the same country we do, breathe the same air and drink the same water, but as a group they are much healthier.

* * *

A huge percentage of people in hospitals are there because of lifestyle and habit. As little as five percent of cancers are the result of genetics – meaning the other 95 percent are from self-inflicted lifestyle choices or from living in unhealthy conditions.

I know this from experience, because almost every time I've been in the hospital as an adult, it was attributed to lifestyle. I survived a heart attack, and now I'm coping with the rare blood disease citrullinemia. The blood disease is not my fault – it's genetic and I'm one of the one in 200,000 unlucky people in the United States to have this thing – but my heart attack was the result of a blocked artery that was attributed to my not eating well, not exercising enough and smoking four or five cigars a day.

These were self-inflicted wounds.

I was shocked into making lifestyle changes. I no longer smoke or drink, and I maintain my weight. I can live another 20 years, which is a normal lifespan today. The sad thing is, about one in four people makes no changes to his or her lifestyle even after a catastrophic event such as a heart attack or stroke.

We've got to stop doing stupid things to ourselves!

The first step to ending self-inflicted wounds is the admission that you have a problem. Otherwise, you'll be like me and probably will be admitted to a hospital.

Another key is preventative healthcare, like getting a flu shot and an annual physical, and getting treated early for things such as heart disease. If you have good insurance or a lot of money, you can do this because you have access to advice and doctors, and you'll probably have a good outcome. But if you're poor and you wait until you're really sick to visit the emergency room, usually the outcome won't be so good.

Plus, it costs a lot more to treat a sick person than to prevent the person from getting sick in the first place. That's why the Affordable Care Act provides incentives for preventative care – because it saves money in the long run.

But how do we stop inflicting wounds on others and make sure people don't end up in the hospital too early? One way is to provide everyone with clean drinking water and clean air to reduce the epidemic of upper respiratory illness. As a culture, we've also got to stop feeding our kids candy and sodas made with 15 spoons of sugar!

We know all this, yet we keep hurting ourselves and others. We keep polluting and we keep smoking and eating and drinking more of the wrong stuff.

One of the indications that we are not raising a healthy generation is that so many young people are not eligible for military service. More than 70 percent of 17- to 24-year-olds do not qualify for military service, and the major reason is obesity. Of those who qualify, more than half cannot pass a basic physical test, which is no doubt related to the fact that only six states today require schools to teach physical education from kindergarten to 12th grade.

Obesity isn't just a health issue that can lead to heart problems and diabetes. It's a national security issue, because the pool of eligible candidates for military service grows smaller every year.

*   *   *

What we need is a huge cultural shift in health. We've already seen it happen with the Surgeon General's report on smoking in 1964 that linked smoking to diseases like lung cancer and emphysema. That shocking announcement led to a dramatic decrease in tobacco use, and the reduction in smoking saved untold lives.

While this was going on, though, Marlboro cigarettes came up with an amazing piece of advertising history. The Marlboro Man was a cool dude. When I rode my horse, I tried to replicate that look. He had a great horse, all the cool clothes, a nice-looking hat, and he was out there puffing on a Marlboro. Interestingly, the actor who played the Marlboro Man died of lung cancer from smoking.

When I was a major in the Army at Fort Leavenworth, the back of each classroom was for the smokers, and there was always a smoking section on airplanes. How stupid was that? We were all breathing the same polluted air in a confined space! At least we know now that breathing second-hand smoke is almost as bad for us as smoking.

We also had a cultural shift with AIDS, which was once thought of as the "gay disease" but which became a global epidemic. When I was serving in Germany, my daughter Stefanie came home from school one day and said, "Dad, we need to talk about AIDS." It shocked me, because she was only nine years old, but they were already educating the kids – which ultimately saved lives because everyone had an understanding of the disease and how to avoid contracting it. There were also public service announcements on TV, and Hollywood got involved and made movies about it.

That's what we need to do with our own health. We all know that soda is full of sugar and that a good amount of fast food is unhealthy, so it's up to us to take charge.

For some reason, it's acceptable to gain weight and joke about it or to drink until you fall over and laugh about it. Being obese or living an unhealthy lifestyle has become socially acceptable, and that's a problem.

We've got to stop doing stupid things to ourselves – because healthcare is not just what doctors can do for you, it's what you can do for yourself.

Healthcare is a basic human right

The failings of the healthcare system really came into focus for me the Sunday after Hurricane Katrina hit in 2005, when I flew to the New Orleans airport to meet Secretary of Defense Donald Rumsfeld and Chairman of the Joint Chiefs of Staff General Richard Myers. I got there a few minutes early, so I walked through the concourses at the airport to see what was going on.

Those concourses were full of old people who had been evacuated from nursing homes. I still get goose bumps when I think about that scene: all those old people lying on cots, wearing smocks that looked like someone took a sack and cut out holes for the arms and neck. It was like something you'd see in the Third World.

The doctors and nurses told me they could do more for these people if they knew where their health records were. All they knew were their names. One nurse told me she asked a 93-year-old lady what medications she was taking.

"Baby, I'm on that little red pill," she said.

We can put a man on the moon, but all we knew about this little old lady was that she took a little red pill. This is the real impact of not having medical records.

How hard would it have been for the nursing homes to place some sort of band or something on these old people, so we'd know who they were and what drugs they were taking?

Those old people were fortunate to get out when their nursing homes flooded. But why in the world would anyone build a nursing home inside a flood zone? That's bad enough, but then they had no escape plan. These were human beings, but they were being treated worse than cattle.

I looked at this scene, and I thought, *So, this is where you end up if you're lucky. If you don't end up like this, you died young.*

That is the ultimate in stupidity, and it hurt my heart.

* * *

For too many people like the elderly and the poor, healthcare is a commodity that you get only if you can afford it. If you can't get through that door, you can't get treated. The challenge is how to get into the system, especially if you're a Medicare patient or a poor person who relies on Medicaid.

When I went from being insured through the military to being a retiree and signing up for Medicare, I was shocked to find out they wanted me to pay more than $400 a month for Medicare Part B, which is medical insurance – and the same amount again for my wife. My mother-in-law pays only about $100 a month because the amount is based on income.

I paid into Social Security my entire life, so why was I being told I had to pay again? It comes down to costs, which, they tell us, have risen faster than Medicare can absorb. Without the extra insurance, Medicare will go broke – and then we're all screwed.

Now, every month my Part B deduction just comes right out of my Social Security check. It's only fair that if you're still working and have income, you pay a little more. It doesn't bother me. I'm not missing any meals or cutting the budget because of what I have to pay, and I get good medical care.

I'm blessed just to be working, but there are many people who are not as fortunate.

I feel strongly that healthcare is a human right, but too many people in the United States aren't given that right. The Affordable Care Act ended up being highly successful in extending that right to millions of people, but the rollout was a failure. If we flew our airplanes like that, they would all wreck. If we were trying to fly to the moon, we would miss it. How in the 21st century could we screw up something this badly? It's because the politicians hired the wrong people with the wrong skills to roll out one of the most anticipated social programs since the Franklin D. Roosevelt years and the beginning of Social Security in 1935.

While this was going on, the political class that raised hell about the Affordable Care Act and its cost thought it was just fine to spend billions of dollars overseas to fight piss-ant wars that don't make a difference to the security of the people we are supposedly fighting for. They don't argue about spending money overseas, only about the money we spend on ourselves for basic human rights like healthcare.

This is one of the biggest dilemmas of our lifetime, and nobody should have to make the decision between paying the rent or seeing the doctor. In the wealthiest nation on Earth, all of us should be able to see a doctor without worrying about how to pay for the visit.

* * *

On a related note, businesses need to do a better job of accommodating sick employees. Many people can't afford to stay home, even for a day – but you should stay home if you're sick, instead of making everyone else sick!

When I was young, I used to hear my mom talk about how some of our ancestors died of "yellow jack" – what most people call yellow fever. It was pretty common in the South in the 1700s and 1800s until they figured out that the disease was carried by mosquitoes. It went away because we controlled the mosquitoes and developed a vaccine, but the disease still exists and there's no saying it won't come back. It's somewhere out there in the swamps.

Because of the danger of something like yellow fever coming back, or an outbreak of Ebola, we can't afford for people *not* to go to the doctor if they're sick. It is a national security issue, and it can happen quickly. Disease moves at the speed of a jet plane.

* * *

We can solve all these issues if we simply stop doing stupid things, and if we take care of our citizens and make healthcare affordable for everyone. We must recognize, once and for all, the basic truth that healthcare is a human right – not just for individuals, but for the health and safety of our nation.

—— *Calls to action* ——

1. Eat right, quit smoking, and drink only in moderation (if at all).

2. Exercise more.

3. Stop giving sugar to children every time they open their mouths.

4. Remember that healthcare is a right, not a privilege.

5. Stop over-prescribing prescription drugs.

6. Don't keep making the same mistakes ... don't get stuck on stupid!

Chapter 9

Clean water is our lifeblood

Two things are infinite: the universe and human stupidity. And I'm not sure about the universe.

– Albert Einstein

he next major international wars will be fought for water.

For the past few decades, the biggest threat to global security has been competition for oil. But now it's about water.

In fact, it's already happening. There's been a sustained drought in parts of Africa and the Middle East for many years, and this has put a strain on governments to find new sources of water.

Some analysts claim the Syrian war, which began in 2011, was started over competition for water. In the Middle East, nations like Israel, Jordan and their neighbors are always in conflict over who controls the water.

Water has become a commercial commodity that in many respects is more valuable than oil. Consider that about 60 percent of the human body is water, and that clean drinking water is our lifeblood. We also use massive amounts of water to produce the food we need in order to survive.

Oil, on the other hand, is somewhat of a luxury, and we're finding ways to replace it.

Since the 19th century, water has evolved from being a public commodity to a private enterprise. However, it may be difficult to realize that water – like oil – has become "monetized," because it seems like water is everywhere. We're surrounded by it; we take it for granted.

Nonetheless, we can pay more for water than we do for gasoline. A gallon of gasoline costs $2 to $3. At the airport, a 20-ounce bottle of water costs $4 – which works out to about $25 a gallon. And it comes from places like Fiji or Iceland.

Why in the hell are we importing water from Fiji? That's a drought-stricken country run by a dysfunctional military regime and where the citizens struggle to find clean drinking water. Why? $25 a gallon, that's why! It's more valuable than oil. There's money to be made with water.

Clean drinking water is a human right

Consider that there is less clean water in the world today than there was yesterday, and there will be

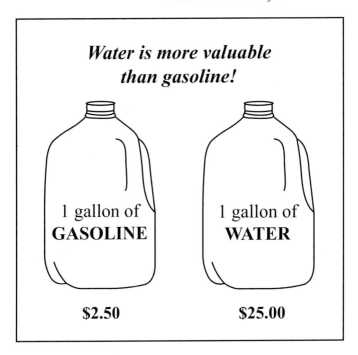

Water is more valuable than gasoline!

1 gallon of **GASOLINE** — $2.50

1 gallon of **WATER** — $25.00

Believe it or not, water can be more expensive than gasoline. In fact, when bought in a 20-ounce bottle in an airport, water sells for $4.00; this works out to more than $25.00 per gallon. Gasoline sells for one-tenth that amount, or $2.50 per gallon.

even less tomorrow. The reason is the growing global population and the strain this puts on all resources.

Between 1997 and 2017, we grew from about 5.8 billion people to 7.5 billion people, and the growing population keeps dirtying the water but not cleaning it. The speculation is that the world will grow to 10 billion people by 2067. This growth will create an even greater requirement for more clean water and more food.

Food production consumes a lot of water from an agricultural perspective, and a lot of that water gets polluted as we use it to grow those big fat pork chops and steaks, raise juicy hens, and produce ever more abundant harvests of corn, wheat, oats and other grains. Believe it or not, it takes about 660 gallons of water to produce all the ingredients in a single hamburger.

It's widely known that the United States has less than five percent of the world's population, though we consume 25 percent of the world's resources. In population rankings, the U.S. is number three behind China and India – each of which has more than 1.3 billion people. Each of those two countries has a billion more people than we have.

I look at this through a military lens, and I see the threat we are facing when the world goes from 7.5 billion people to 10 billion. The expanded global population is going to require at least 33 percent more food than what we're producing now. Moreover, in the world today, more than a billion people don't have electricity and another 700 million don't have clean water in their homes.

Again, we have less clean drinking water today than we had yesterday or will have tomorrow because we're consuming it and we're dirtying it, but we're not cleaning it.

The three most obvious ways we're not taking care of our water are:

• We're still allowing garbage to be dumped into our oceans.

• We're allowing our coastal aquifers to be destroyed through oil and gas production.

• We're allowing the over-use of fertilizers for agricultural production.

The explosion of the global population over the past 50 years came about partly because people gained greater access to clean water. Much of the progress in this area is due to well-thought-out initiatives by the U.S. government and organizations like the Peace Corps that work with non-governmental organizations to show people in developing nations how to clean their water and how to avoid polluting it. The adoption of better sanitation practices has also been a critical component of this progress.

We have to embrace technology to find solutions

Manufacturing and farming consumes a tremendous amount of water. We know the importance of good farming practices and the impact they continue to make on our economy and on our ability to feed ourselves and help feed the rest of the world. But we're going to have to come up with some better solutions to the agricultural runoff.

Many of us have lived on farms, as I have, or have farmers who are relatives and friends. So I understand

'*We're not taking care of our water. We're still allowing garbage to be dumped into our oceans. We're allowing our coastal aquifers to be destroyed through oil and gas production. We're allowing the over-use of fertilizers for agricultural production.* '

many of the challenges that farmers have to deal with.

At the same time, we're still doing stupid things with farming and water – and that's got to change.

In the early months of 2017, I was at a conference at Tulane University in New Orleans where they were looking for a solution to the "dead zone" in the Gulf of Mexico. The "dead zone" is an area of about 8,000 square miles off the Louisiana coast west of the Mississippi River delta where oxygen in the water is so depleted that the water cannot support life. This occurs from the spring through the fall.

The culprit is the nutrient-rich discharge from the Atchafalaya River and Mississippi River – in other words, excess fertilizer in the agricultural runoff from 31 states that flows into the rivers and eventually into the Gulf of Mexico. Other components of this discharge include eroded soil, animal waste and sewage.

To help find a solution to the "dead zone," Taylor Energy Co. of New Orleans put forth a grant of

$1 million. (Ironically, one of the company's offshore oil wells has been leaking hundreds of gallons of oil every day into the Gulf of Mexico since it was heavily damaged during Hurricane Ivan in 2004. Efforts to stem the flow have failed.)

The "dead zone" is just one example of the damage we've been doing to our water. And we've been abusing it for a long, long time – at least 50 years that I know of.

But what can we do about it? How can we reverse this trend?

First, we have to embrace technology to find solutions, and one of the most important ideas is to determine how much fertilizer the farmers really need in order to optimize the production of their crops.

What we've discovered is that farmers are able to reduce the amount of fertilizer they need by up to 40 percent simply by testing the soil frequently and monitoring crop growth. It's all done based on data collected from the fields that tells the farmer he can reduce the amount of fertilizer he uses and still get the same production per acre. That's pretty cool! The rest of that fertilizer is wasted; it's nothing but excess that ends up in the rivers and then in the Gulf of Mexico.

We still have to address the toxic runoff from things like pig and chicken farms, but we're getting a better understanding of how to tackle this problem.

It's an overstatement of the obvious, but we've got to stop doing stupid things to our water. We've

The Cuyahoga River in Ohio was so polluted that it actually caught fire in 1969. Federal environmental protection legislation soon followed.

got to stop dirtying and poisoning it. And we've got to clean the water that we're dirtying. Our very lives depend on it – seriously.

The good old days ...
when rivers caught on fire

Water is a complex issue, and access to navigable water and drinking water was fundamental to the drawing of boundaries between states in the early history of the United States. The Supreme Court and state supreme courts were frequently involved in settling disputes over water and water rights.

Water is often under-priced, but many of our municipalities have used water as a cash cow – meaning they will charge as much for water as they think the citizens can bear, and they don't always use that money to re-invest in the water system. Instead, they use it to pay other bills.

The cost of clean water is rapidly increasing, and in the not-too-distant future many millions of households in the United States may not be able to afford their water bills.

The most expensive places for water in America are Atlanta and Seattle. A family of four using a typical 100 gallons of water a day pays around $326 per month for water in Atlanta and $310 in Seattle.

At the other end of the scale, the same family living in Los Angeles pays less than half of what they'd pay in Atlanta. In Phoenix, it's one-quarter and in Las Vegas it's one-fifth, or $64. These cities are in deserts, so they have to pipe in all their water. Does this make sense?

Even though access to water is a right, we still have to pay for it in the same way we pay for electricity and highways. Otherwise, sound maintenance of the public water systems would be close to impossible in communities where water is under-priced.

A glaring example of dirty water that really got the public's attention is the Cuyahoga River in northeast Ohio. It was so polluted that it actually caught fire in 1969. This dramatic incident helped to spawn the environmental movement in the 1970s that gave birth to the Clean Water Act, the Safe Drinking Water Act and other regulations designed to help us clean our water.

A more modern example of not keeping our water clean and safe is what happened in Flint, Michigan.

This was a comedy of errors. First of all, General

Motors in Flint and elsewhere produced cars with lead-compatible engines, which led to the Flint River being polluted with lead. The lead in the water ran through the city's pipes for so many years that the Flint water system became a maintenance problem, to put it mildly.

The bureaucrats switched the city's water from the Flint River to Detroit city water, but that exacerbated the problem because it dislodged the lead in the pipes. Now we have a city where the water system is full of lead and most of the population drinks only bottled or filtered water.

It's not just Flint, though. It's happening elsewhere as well. One of the worst water systems in the nation is in Martin County, Kentucky, a coal-mining region where dirty water is a way of life and people dare not drink it.

In Louisiana, the small community of St. Joseph has a water system that is deteriorating and the disgusting brown water is contaminated with lead and copper. People have to buy their own drinking water. It's costing about $9 million to fix just this one system for about 500 homes. At the same time, the residents can't afford to pay high water bills to make the system workable into the future.

Another problem city in Louisiana is Ville Platte, which is also plagued with brown, polluted drinking water. People there tell me things like, "We're not drinking that water," and "I'm not going to come back here and raise children with that water."

It's worth noting that bad water in places like St. Joseph and Ville Platte is contributing to the death of small towns.

* * *

We've made great progress over the years, but today it's almost like we've come full circle with so many politicians and industry lobbyists whining about over-regulating industry. We didn't over-regulate industry. We had rivers on fire and we poisoned entire cities! The air was so dirty in some cities, you couldn't see from one side of the street to the other.

One of the first pieces of legislation signed by Donald Trump when he became President in 2017 was one repealing a regulation that stopped coal-mining companies from dumping waste and toxic coal ash into streams and rivers.

What the hell's going on that we need to make our rivers dirtier again? Does the Trump administration really know what they are doing by telling mining companies it's okay to let their runoff go straight into the rivers and streams? Did we learn nothing from the Cuyahoga River fire and the other disasters we've seen in our lifetime?

Water is big business

The competition between industry and the public over access to water is readily evident in Louisiana, where there are three major aquifers: The Chicot

Aquifer in southwestern Louisiana, the Sparta Aquifer in northern Louisiana, and the Southern Hills Aquifer that serves five parishes around Baton Rouge.

Just two companies in Baton Rouge – ExxonMobil and Georgia Pacific – use more water every day from the Southern Hills Aquifer than all the people and all the other industries in those five parishes put together. ExxonMobil uses about 23 million gallons a day from this aquifer and Georgia-Pacific uses 34 million gallons.

These companies can do it legally because of the "right of capture" that says if you have water underneath your land you can capture it. (On the other hand, if you have oil underneath your land you don't necessarily own it and you don't always have the right to capture it.)

The position of these two companies is this: "We're citizens too. We've got a right to that water." Meanwhile, other companies – Shell Oil and Dow Chemical, for example – use Mississippi River water. But ExxonMobil and Georgia-Pacific insist on using aquifer water – which is also the drinking water for five parishes – because they say the shift from aquifer to river water would cost them too much money.

*   *   *

One of the consequences of the overuse of the Southern Hills Aquifer is saltwater intrusion from the Gulf of Mexico. The water pressure in part of the aquifer is relatively low because the aquifer is being drained too quickly; this creates a kind of capillary action that draws the Gulf of Mexico's saltwater into the aquifer. It's a natural process; the saltwater is moving up towards Baton Rouge. When the level of salt in the water becomes too high, the water will be undrinkable.

Then what?

The State Legislature, which is influenced by industry lobbyists, takes the position that if we run short of water from the aquifer, we'll just drink out of the Mississippi River, as is the practice in New Orleans. The reason they drink the river water is that there's too much saltwater in their local aquifer.

Another example of industry affecting the aquifers that provide drinking water can be found in Miami, Florida. This city gets most of its drinking water from the upper Biscayne Aquifer. However, waste and untreated sewage are dumped into the nearby Floridan Aquifer, and there are plans to add radioactive waste to the mixture. Studies have shown that this waste could seep into the Biscayne Aquifer.

Problems in the 'Chemical Corridor'

One of the problem areas for clean water is the "Chemical Corridor" between Houston and New Orleans; it's dotted with refineries that use huge quantities of chemicals and hazardous materials. These refineries also consume a vast amount of water – and they create a lot of dirty water.

I once got into an argument about an industrial plant that was planned for a city right in the middle of the corridor, Lake Charles, Louisiana. The plant planned to use 14 million gallons of water a day, which would be discharged as warm water into the Calcasieu River after going through the industrial process. One of the effects of doing that is that the fish in the river could be born either all male or all female, because temperature affects the fish population and the sex of the fish. As a result, sooner or later, there could be no fish left.

Nonetheless, one of the big supporters of this project was the leader of the local Chamber of Commerce. He slapped me on the shoulder at a meeting.

"General, this is going to be great!" he said.

"Oh, I don't think so," I said, then I pointed out how the plant would pollute the river.

"Well, General, we don't drink the water here. We use bottled water," he replied.

He was speaking from the heart, but he had become brainwashed to the idea that it was more important to have an industrial plant than clean water – and that the logical solution wasn't to try to stop the pollution but to drink bottled water.

Clean water is a human right. But we have been hoodwinked by elected officials who try to convince us that everything should take a back seat to growing the economy. Their defense is that polluting the water system and making the water unfit to drink is an acceptable consequence of creating jobs.

Well, okay, but is the creation of a few jobs or even a few hundred jobs worth 72,000 people in Lake Charles – and many more beyond – having to drink bottled water?

The purpose of the government is to serve the people, period.

As with many other aspects of our society, the concept of democracy in the way we deal with water has been subverted. State and city water boards and water commissions across the nation have become a lot like every other political body.

The idea of our democracy when we won our freedom in 1776 was that the people we elected would look after us and our communities. What's happened is that the people who run for office are dependent on political donors who expect something in return. Too many politicians have continued to erode the basic principle that the purpose of government is to serve the people; too often, it appears that the purpose of government is to serve business, and the business of water is no different from any other.

In late 2016 and early 2017, there were several controversial oil pipelines that were proposed to run through areas that could be significantly harmed by oil spills, should they occur. A spill from the Keystone XL pipeline in the Midwest could poison the Ogallala Aquifer, which provides drinking water for about two million people and which makes the

Midwest the "breadbasket of the nation."

If the Ogallala Aquifer were to become unusable, the agricultural economy would collapse and two million people would be drinking bottled water.

*   *   *

The system we are fighting against is very, very entrenched in politics. You could go to Texas, California or just about anywhere, and you'd find the same problems. Even though water should be protected as a human right, we've allowed it to be monetized, or commercialized. It's not just that we are over-using the water, it's that we're failing to clean it.

Wherever you deal with water, there is a tight-knit group of politicians who know ways to circumvent regulations like the Clean Water Act. Before he was Vice President, Dick Cheney was CEO of Halliburton, the company that patented hydraulic fracturing, better known as "fracking." This process injects massive amounts of hazardous chemicals into the ground – often adjacent to underground drinking water supplies – in order to squeeze out a few more barrels of oil.

In 2001, Vice President Cheney chaired a special task force that recommended to the Environmental Protection Agency (EPA) that fracking should be exempt from the Safe Drinking Water Act. In a decision known as the "Halliburton Loophole," the EPA declared that fracking poses "little or no threat" to drinking water.

Conveniently, the EPA simply ignored information that unregulated fracking can be hazardous to human health and that the fluids utilized in the process can contaminate drinking water long after the drilling has ended. We've experienced other dramatic results of fracking, as well: frequent earthquakes in places like Oklahoma that rarely had them before fracking, and drinking water that catches on fire right out of the faucet.

This started in the George W. Bush Administration, but the Barack Obama Administration had eight years to fix it. They didn't fix it, because they thought it would slow down economic growth if they declared fracking chemicals to be hazardous. As a result, people can now dump fracking water straight into rivers and the Gulf of Mexico, adding to the problems we already face with the "dead zone."

We've got to stop doing stupid things like this. If you dirty the water, you're responsible for cleaning it.

Cultural shift needed
to make water clean again

As private citizens, we want clean drinking water. But this goal is undermined by a few companies that refuse to clean the water they use. That's not defensible, and the damage that's being done is long-term. When we allow places like the Gulf of Mexico to be polluted, we're not going to see that turn around quickly.

We need a cultural shift when it comes to our attitudes about water, just like we had with smoking and AIDS. The cultural shift is happening in parts of California, where they made the price of water such that people have to pay dearly to get a green front yard. In the 1990s, I lived for a while at Fort Irwin near Barstow in California's Mojave Desert, and everyone had desert lawns with zero- or low-moisture requirements.

At the same time that California is leading this cultural shift, though, their farmers continue to grow crops that need huge amounts of water. It takes about five gallons of water to produce each and every walnut and more than a gallon for every almond.

We need to take the lessons we learned from smoking and AIDS and say, "OK, we had a cultural shift with them, and now we've got to stop being stupid with water."

Everybody needs to buy into the fact that we are responsible for our actions. There are always "save the water" events that focus on what we the people can do in our own homes, like taking shorter showers and not over-watering our lawns – but they never focus on the big industries that are the biggest culprits.

The first thing we've got to do is educate the people, because a lot of people don't understand that we've got a water problem and that it's getting worse by the day. As I noted earlier, it's not obvious that we're on the brink of a catastrophe, because we're surrounded by water.

Clearly, a lot of damage was done to our water resources over the past 50 years. So, what will it be like in another 50 years? We need a long-range, global perspective on water, because as the population grows and sea levels rise, we're going to have less arable land to raise more food for more people. We've got to be smarter about water.

——— *Calls to action* ———

1. Reduce water consumption.

2. Fight to enforce the Clean Water Act and Safe Drinking Water Act.

3. Create technology that can clean water more efficiently.

4. Reduce fertilizer use on farms.

5. Don't let private companies subvert the public's right to clean drinking water.

6. Don't keep making the same mistakes ... don't get stuck on stupid!

The severe flooding of Denham Springs, La., in August of 2016 is a good example of what can happen when man disrupts the natural flow of water in a floodplain. Much of the city was under four to six feet of water following a 24-inch rainfall. The flooding was partly due to the fact that a concrete barrier – built as a safety measure between opposing lanes of traffic on nearby I-12 – interfered with the drainage of the city.

Chapter 10

The consequences of messing with Mother Nature

*Never underestimate the power
of stupid people in large groups.*

– George Carlin

When I was a young boy, there was some land not far from our farm that I thought would be perfect for my 4-H farm projects. We could also raise hay there. One day, I was riding around with my grandfather, and I told him I thought we should buy that land.

He disagreed.

"Boy, let me tell you something. In 1927, that land was under 13 feet of water."

He was talking about the Great Mississippi River Flood of 1927 that saw the river overflow its banks and flood 27,000 square miles from Illinois through Louisiana.

We didn't buy that land, but if you go to that exact same place now, it's full of mega-mansions. Everyone who lives there knows they're in a flood plain, and it's just a matter of time before they flood again and the water is 13 feet deep again.

Is that stupid, or what?

I learned a valuable lesson from my grandfather before it was too late, but some people unfortunately have to learn from experience. Today, people don't always know if they're in a flood zone, and several have asked me about it.

"How do I know if I'm in a flood zone?"

My answer is that if you can see water from your house, you're in a flood zone.

If you walk onto your porch and you say, "Wow, that's a beautiful river," you live in a flood zone.

If the community you're in is named after water, you're in a flood zone!

If you live in a city like Great Falls or Daytona Beach or on a street named "River Road" or "Ocean Drive," you're in a flood zone.

After the September 2013 floods in Colorado, I was talking to Colorado Governor John Hickenlooper about how we build resiliency.

"Governor, one of the aspects of resiliency is that you have to stop putting oil pipelines and fracking wells inside old river basins, because they get damaged in floods and contaminate the floodwaters," I said.

"Well, General, that's why we put the wells there.

'*How do you know if you're in a flood zone?*

If you can see water from your house, you're in a flood zone. If the community you're in is named after water, you're in a flood zone! If you live in a city like Great Falls or Daytona Beach or on a street named "River Road" or "Ocean Drive," you're in a flood zone! '

They haven't flooded before," he said.

"You've gotta be kidding me! How do you think the river basins got there?" I replied.

With the never-ending growth in population, we're building in places where we never built before, and the change in the global climate means that flooding has become more common and more severe. Yet, we look the other way and pretend to be surprised when river basins flood or River Road becomes part of the river.

The sweetheart deals that keep us poor

We've lost so much of the Gulf of Mexico's coastal wetlands over the last 50 years that a Katrina-like hurricane in Louisiana could create a surge that pushes surface water about 30 to 40 miles inland. In fact, the "Chemical Corridor" between New Orleans and Houston has been designated by the Federal government as one big flood zone below I-10.

Most of the wetlands in Louisiana are owned by industry, and the reason we got into this ecological trouble is the construction of pipelines and oil exploration canals that have allowed saltwater intrusion. When this happens, it causes an ecological imbalance that kills the wetlands. Saltwater causes plants to die, and it's the plants' roots that keep the land together. Without the plants and their roots, the land just washes away.

*   *   *

It started in 1849 and 1850 when the Federal government donated about 8.5 million acres of swamps and wetlands to the State of Louisiana through the Swamp Acts; in turn, the State sold the land for as little as 12.5 cents an acre to help finance land reclamation and the construction of levees along the Mississippi River.

Churches, private companies and investors throughout the United States bought Louisiana's wetlands, and for the most part they were absentee landlords.

The wetlands serve as natural reservoirs for floodwaters and as buffers that absorb the energy of hurricanes and rebuff the tidal surge. But it's been well documented that Louisiana is losing about a football field's worth of wetlands every hour of every day. That's about 2,000 square miles lost in 80 years – since 1937 – or, an area greater than the state of Rhode

Island! It's the fastest-disappearing land in the world.

Those 2,000 square miles used to be part of Louisiana, but now they're part of the Gulf of Mexico.

There's a stipulation in Louisiana law that if the land becomes covered by water and is therefore navigable, it returns to the ownership of the State. Landowners don't want to lose their land, so they're blocking it off and putting up "No Entry" signs so you and I can't go there and see that it's covered by water. There are other ways to check, but the best way to find out if a swamp is navigable is to go there and see for yourself.

Of course, it's not the land that's the issue. The land and the resources *underneath* are supposed to be returned to the State, and what's *underneath* is oil and gas. And there are still a lot of wells that are producing a lot of income from what's underneath the surface.

The loss of our wetlands is a double-edged sword. As a result of the loss of wetlands, which are a key to preventing flooding along our coasts, the storms are coming ashore stronger. This, in turn, exacerbates not only the loss of land in coastal Louisiana but the loss of homes, recreational camps and roads. We saw this with hurricanes Katrina, Gustav, Irene and Ike, which pushed water deep into Plaquemines, Terrebonne and Cameron parishes.

*   *   *

Inside of Cameron Parish, in the southwest corner

of Louisiana, you'll find the Miami Corporation land reserve, which is made up of thousands of acres of wetlands. The owners' family and friends come here to hunt ducks. They also sublease the land to private hunting and fishing clubs, and they post signs because they don't want anybody else in there. The hunting and fishing clubs hire armed guards to discourage trespassing.

And because it's wetlands, commercial enterprises such as the Miami Corporation, ExxonMobil, Chevron and other large corporations pay as little as 50 cents an acre in property tax.

The greatest value of the land reserve, of course, is the oil and gas they are taking from it.

When I was out in California doing a lecture for the Southern California Gas Company (or SoCalGas, as it's known), I asked them where their gas comes from. SoCalGas is the nation's largest natural gas distribution utility, with more than 21 million customers in southern California, including Los Angeles.

They told me they get their gas from Cameron Parish, Louisiana. In essence, a drilling rig takes the gas from the ground and the landowner pays a modest severance tax – plus as little as 50 cents an acre in property tax – then the gas is piped out to California.

What a business plan! The State of Louisiana gets next to nothing in the deal and SoCalGas makes a nice profit selling our natural resources to its customers.

Louisiana is the third-largest energy producer in the nation, and it should be one of the richest states.

But our brilliant politicians have made all these sweet-heart deals and have practically given away our natural resources, so we're one of the poorest states and we can't even adequately fund our schools and hospitals.

That's not just stupid, it's damn stupid!

It's not that we don't generate wealth here in Louisiana. It's that we don't keep it because of the exceptions and exemptions to tax. We continue to allow our wealth to leave the state.

We are literally subsidizing multi-national corporations that make billions of dollars in profits while we here in Louisiana are cutting funds from education and hospitals.

In total, there's up to $300 million more that the State of Louisiana could be collecting in oil and gas revenues every year. Meanwhile, the State Legislature is trying to figure out how to make up a $300 million deficit. That shouldn't be so difficult, given the amount of wealth this state creates for lage corporations.

This can be fixed, but we keep looking in the wrong places and we keep doing business in a stupid way.

The consequences of disrupting flood plains and wetlands

About 40 percent of the U.S. population lives near the coast, and that number goes up each time the census is taken. Millions more live near rivers, because water was key not only for drinking but for industrialization and transportation in the good old days. Where the water was, that's where the cities went. People have an infatuation with water; it has a calming effect.

One of the unintended consequences of widespread construction, combined with climate change and the rise in sea levels, is what has become known as "nuisance flooding."

In August 2016, the city of Denham Springs, La., a few miles east of Baton Rouge on I-12, was devastated by the floods that inundated Louisiana following rainfall that exceeded 24 inches in some areas. The key word in the town's name is "Springs." It's evident from the name alone that it's in a flood plain.

When you move into a flood plain and disrupt the natural flow of water, somebody's going to flood unintentionally – and that's exactly what happened in August 2016.

Much of I-12 is elevated above the ground, which allows floodwater to flow underneath and follow the path of least resistance it has followed for thousands of years towards the swamps and the Gulf of Mexico. Denham Springs is north of I-12, but the road at that point is not elevated.

When improvements were made to the Interstate, the contractors couldn't widen the road to add lanes without taking more private property, so they took out the median and put in new lanes. With the median gone, they put a tall concrete divider wall down the middle as a safety barrier between the eastbound and westbound traffic.

In August 2016, the water that normally would have flowed south from Denham Springs through, under and over the Interstate was blocked by this wall. That was a huge contributing factor to much of Denham Springs being under four to six feet of water – and a clear example of what happens when we disrupt the wetlands and the flood plains.

*　*　*

After Hurricane Katrina in 2005, many people decided to move out of New Orleans and into new subdivisions on the north shore of Lake Pontchartrain, the large lake that sits north of New Orleans. The north shore was also affected by Katrina, but the damage was minimal compared to what happened to New Orleans.

One of those places is Slidell, which is northeast of New Orleans, where I-10 and I-12 meet, just a few miles from the Mississippi border. Slidell has seen a significant increase in population, and they had to put streets and houses in the wetlands to accommodate all the people. What's going to happen the next time we get a storm surge in the lake is that the water is going to have an easy path down those nice paved streets – and those new subdivisions will be flooded.

In the mid-1960s, New Orleans itself was made more vulnerable to storm surges because of the creation of the Mississippi River-Gulf Outlet canal, better known as MR-GO and pronounced "Mister Go." It's a man-made problem, just like the many other industrial canals that were built in the wetlands. These canals bring saltwater directly into the wetlands, and MR-GO is one of the worst offenders.

MR-GO was built because powerful U.S. Rep. Lindy Boggs wanted it built, ostensibly as a shortcut for ships going to New Orleans. But what she and her pals really wanted to do was develop the land along MR-GO for hunting clubs and resorts. The plan was for a whole lot of industrial and mixed-use development.

From the day it was built, though, ships never used MR-GO because weird currents meant that captains couldn't control their ships. This is what happens when you make political decisions instead of practical ones. MR-GO was originally 650 feet wide, but the intrusion of saltwater killed the vegetation, making the canal much wider – and forming a perfect funnel that enabled the storm surge to reach New Orleans during Hurricane Katrina.

The water rushing up MR-GO inundated the Ninth Ward and contributed to the flooding of New Orleans. Fortunately, MR-GO was closed after Katrina and a $1 billion surge barrier was built to prevent future storm surges from reaching New Orleans. It's exactly like closing the barn door after the horse is out.

Oil and water don't mix

There are about 125,000 miles of oil and gas pipelines in Louisiana, which is enough to go around the world five times. The pipeline network has evolved over the years, and much of it goes through the wetlands and swamps, including through the Atchafalaya River Basin in south Louisiana. This basin is the largest river swamp in the United States; it was declared a National Heritage Area in 2006 during the George W. Bush administration.

Some of the pipelines in the Atchafalaya – as well as oil and gas wells – were built prior to the Clean Water Act of 1972. After the Clean Water Act, oil and gas companies had to pay particular attention to protecting our water sources, but there were basically no rules before that.

For some reason, the Corps of Engineers has stated that even though the wells and pipelines were not put in to meet current standards, the Corps doesn't have the authority to enforce compliance with current law. Because of this and the ineptness of politicians who made no effort to protect the land, the Atchafalaya Basin swampland is deteriorating. It's certainly not destroyed – it's still a magnificent place – but it's not the place it was before we put all those wells and pipelines in there.

The water in the basin naturally wants to run north to south, but most of the pipelines through it go east and west, towards the refineries. When they put many of the pipelines in, they didn't follow the same rules as when, say, they went through a sugarcane field.

You can drive by a sugarcane field or a school playground and see little sticks coming out of the ground showing where the underground pipeline is.

In other words, they filled the trenches and put the land back to the way it was before, and you can safely walk or drive on it. In the Atchafalaya Basin, however, they dug a huge trench and left the spoil on the sides instead of putting it back and restoring the land.

Some of those spoils are 15 feet high, and they look and act like levees. Remember, they are going east-west, so they disturb the natural north-south flow of water.

* * *

Even the newer pipelines aren't without controversy. The proposed Bayou Bridge Pipeline across the Atchafalaya Basin could have a negative effect on our water. There is an average of one new oil spill per day from pipelines nationwide, and a major project like the Bayou Bridge Pipeline could lead to a significant oil spill in the heart of the Atchafalaya Basin.

There was a public hearing about this pipeline, and at least 75 percent of the people there were against it because of its threat to the water in the Atchafalaya Basin. Even though it was a public meeting, it was controlled by the forces that wanted the pipeline built for political or economic gain – with little or no regard for what it might do to the water.

Elected officials were allowed to speak first. Six legislators in suits walked in at the very beginning and spoke eloquently about how safe the pipeline would be and how much they believed in it. They claimed it was about jobs, even though it would create only about

12 full-time jobs. Then, they all left before anyone had a chance to speak against the pipeline.

To their detriment, I spoke about 45 minutes later.

"Where are the legislators? This is a public hearing. They didn't even stick around to hear what you had to say. But I can tell you where they are. They are at Ruth's Chris right now being treated to steaks by the very lobbyists that asked them to come here," I said.

Boy, that room just went crazy, because legislators are supposed to serve the public, but they used their position of privilege to speak first and ignored opposing voices. They went there to represent the interests of a company out of Texas, not to represent the people who elected their sorry asses.

They were willing to risk the environmental health of the Atchafalaya Basin for 12 jobs.

* * *

It's not just the Atchafalaya, of course. It's happening all over the wetlands and all over the United States. Two days after Hurricane Katrina hit the Gulf Coast in 2005, I was flying in a helicopter over the wetlands when I saw a rainbow sheen on the water.

"What in the heck is that?" I asked the pilot.

He told me it was oil from oil derricks that were knocked down by the storm. The oil wells, many of which had been abandoned for years, were spilling untold gallons of oil into the wetlands, and there was nothing we could do to stop it. Those wells were everywhere. It doesn't take much oil to kill the wetlands, and that's when I realized we were facing an uphill battle.

On another occasion, in 2011, I was flying over the Atchafalaya Basin swampland with Mayor Mitch Landrieu of New Orleans. We came across an area with a lot of brown water, which is an indication of oil and water trying to mix, and there was a strong odor of benzine that came into the helicopter. All those leaking and broken oil wells and pipelines were being flushed, which contaminated the water.

We have to stop doing this to our water and our wetlands.

* * *

When it comes to the environment, we should be held accountable to the Pottery Barn rule: "You break it, you own it." Well, we've broken the wetlands, so now we own them and it's up to us to fix them.

Much of the lost wetlands are permanently lost – but if we selectively start protecting some places, we might have a fighting chance. Shutting down the MR-GO was a start, but there is a long way to go.

I lived in the Netherlands for two years, and I observed that one of the secrets of that country's success is how they have reclaimed land from the sea to produce new land. But the type of resources it would take to do the same thing in the U.S. is beyond the capacity of Louisiana or any other single state acting on its own. It's a national issue and a Federal responsibility.

In nearly every case, it's a mess when you start fooling with Mother Nature. We've got to stop creating the conditions that make disasters inevitable. We have to work with nature, not against it. When we go against natural laws, like creating unnatural paths for water to follow, we are really pushing the stupid button.

——— *Calls to action* ———

1. Know if you're in a flood zone, and always be prepared for floods.

2. Be resilient and smart: Build at least one foot above the highest known high-water mark.

3. Start collecting reasonable taxes and royalties on oil and gas companies.

4. Stop altering the environment in ways that lead to man-made disasters.

5. Restore the wetlands.

6. Don't keep making the same mistakes ... don't get stuck on stupid!

U.S. soldiers on patrol in the Vietnam countryside make their way across a river during the Vietnam War circa 1969. The U.S. Army is in a constant state of transition, getting better at what it does with each passing generation as threats to national security evolve.

Chapter 11

'Be all you can be': The story of my life

Stupidity is a more dangerous enemy of the good than malice.

– Dietrich Bonhoeffer

I n my junior year at Southern University in 1969, I drove past the airport in Baton Rouge, Louisiana. I was in my ROTC uniform, and I saw a sign for a turkey-shoot. I didn't know what a turkey-shoot was, but I was a pretty good with a rifle, so I went in.

For $1, the sponsoring organization wanted me to shoot at a target, and the best shot would win a side of beef. That seemed like a pretty good deal, so I paid my $1 and shot at the target. A couple of days later, I got a call saying I'd won the beef.

The next day's campus activities included an ROTC parade and drill. In our freshman and sophomore years, all male students at Southern had to be in ROTC because it was a land-grant college. After that, we could elect to stay in and get on the path to receive our Army commissions, and that is what I dearly wanted to do.

I had to look sharp for the parade, so I shined my shoes and had my uniform ironed and starched. After the parade I went to pick up my beef.

The guy who came to load the beef in my car looked at my uniform and was impressed.

"You look good in that uniform. How ya doing at LSU?" he said.

I told him I went to Southern, not LSU.

"Lord, I thought you was a white boy. You're a nigra?" he said.

Until that moment, it didn't occur to me that if the people putting on the turkey-shoot realized who I was, they probably wouldn't have given me a chance to compete.

This incident brought back painful memories of my junior year in high school, when I had a great-looking Jersey heifer. I took her to the parish livestock show. She was a quality animal that could compete with any other cow in the state. When I got there, I discovered that even the cows were segregated according to the race of their owners. That hurt me more than anything else, because my cow had to be in the back of the barn and wasn't given recognition even though she was the finest one there.

Now, this was during the era of the Vietnam War, with people dodging the draft and lying about medical conditions to get out of the service. I'd always wanted to serve my country, and here I was in 1969 in a military uniform and committed to doing my part – but I was still being treated like a second-class citizen. It was a soul-searching moment.

My initial aspiration was to serve my time in the Army then come back to Louisiana and be a dairy farmer. As things worked out, I was thrown in a different direction. I went into the Army as an obligation, but it ended up being a way of life. Lo and behold, four kids, 24 moves and 37 years kinda flew by.

I don't know a better way I could have spent my adult life than being an Army officer. With a few exceptions, I don't regret a day of it. One of the highlights was at the end of my career when, as a minority person and a lieutenant general in charge of the 1st U. S. Army, I was sent to New Orleans right after Hurricane Katrina.

I was born during the Fort Lauderdale Hurricane in 1947, and now, 58 years later, on the streets of New Orleans, I was able to use the skills I had acquired over a lifetime to help my fellow citizens after a hurricane.

Almost to a point, the Army slogan "Be all you can be" is the story of my life. It allowed me to reach my potential. But I must say my proudest achievement came when both of my sons became soldiers.

Perpetual motion, constant progress

Across American society, we see so much that is

wrong – from schools and prisons to the environment and healthcare. There is so much stupidity in the way we accept what is wrong, and the stupidest thing of all is that we keep doing it.

On the other hand, we must be doing something right. Perhaps I'm prejudiced, having spent my career in the Army, but I would point to the Army as an example of an organization in which we can identify our mistakes and learn from them. The Army is by no means perfect, but one of its fundamental philosophies is the concept that if you are not changing, you are falling behind.

From the day I joined the Army in 1971 until the day I retired in 2008, the Army was in a constant state of transition. There has been an expectation throughout history that each new generation was to make the Army better on its watch, and as a general rule that has happened.

*   *   *

In the early 1900s, the U.S. Army went from riding horses to driving tanks and trucks, and by World War II we had a quasi-modernized Army. The Army was integrated in 1948 following the Selective Service Act, so it happened during my lifetime. Unlike much of America, the Army was always developing and was trying to be one step ahead of stupid. Even during the Korean War we learned valuable lessons from being underprepared and overconfident.

By the time I went to the Army Command and General Staff College, in 1983, we had a strong appreciation for history. In fact, in all of our professional development Army schools, we were encouraged to read military history, whether it was ancient conflicts, the Napoleonic Wars in Europe in the early 1800s, the Civil War in the 1860s or 20th century wars and the consequences of using a nuclear weapon.

From an understanding of history, we learn about how to treat people, as well as about battlefield maneuvers and the development of weaponry. In many cases, we didn't get it right, but we learned from our mistakes.

* * *

When I joined the Army in 1971, the armed forces were quickly transitioning from the draft to an all-volunteer force. For the first three years I was in the Army, we never celebrated Armed Forces Day, because we were afraid of the demonstrations that would be held where I was stationed, at Fort Ord in California.

The Army was in turmoil, mostly due to the Vietnam War, and we were hell-bent on writing history from a new perspective. We made some mistakes along the way, but we have to remember that if the Army is not in transition, we need to be worried.

It's still in transition, and we have no room to rest in terms of our national defense. The threats have evolved through the years, from aircraft to drones and from cyber attacks to powerful cameras and hearing devices and other types of things that have been weaponized.

From World War II to Vietnam, we created some of the most sophisticated heavy weapons in history, but we modified from that to weapons of precision that allowed us to send a missile through a specific window in a specific building from two continents away. We can send drones anywhere in the world, but the pilots are sitting in an air-conditioned room in Colorado.

What has remained constant at the heart of the Army is its ability to recruit young people who swear to uphold the Constitution and protect the nation from all enemies, foreign and domestic – and to do it essentially at minimum wage. That's a blessing to our nation.

My big concern is that we have started creating distance between the Army and the civilian population. Since going to an all-volunteer force, fewer people are coming in contact with soldiers, because fewer Americans have friends or relatives in the Army. The percentage of the population serving in the Army has dropped to about one-fourth of what it was in 1971. We are doing more with fewer people.

One problem is the impact this has on sustaining the Army. If we have to grow the Army back up at some point and move from all-volunteer status to all-out mobilization, we will have a hard time filling our ranks – because the majority of young men and women are not physically fit or don't have the right education.

The Army's three major transitions

The Army is continuously changing to adapt to a changing world, and in my lifetime it has undergone three major transitions.

The first was **racial integration**, which took place shortly after World War II. The Army is a reflection of society, but most Americans don't know there were African American units as early as the American Revolution and the Civil War. Even those of us in segregated schools didn't know this, because there was nothing about this in our history books or in the movies.

At the start of World War II, in 1941, we had fewer than 4,000 African Americans in the armed services. By the end of the war, in 1945, more than 1.2 million African Americans had served in uniform – although they served in segregated regiments and were often behind the lines in non-combat units.

One of the exceptions was the Tuskegee Airmen. Although this was a segregated group, it operated one of the most effective fighter squadrons in the war. Just like back home, though, African Americans could not eat in the same mess halls as white American troops, or even in the same mess halls as white prisoners of war.

On the other hand, once the armed services were integrated, they set the standard for society. While Martin Luther King Jr. and others were marching for integration in cities across America, the Army was

President Harry Truman (left) welcomes an African American into the U.S. military following passage of the Selective Service Act of 1948.

already leading the way.

For many Americans, their first meaningful contact with people of other races was in the Army. A lot of white people had never had social interaction with or worked alongside a black person before, and for many black people it was the first time they slept under the same roof or ate in the same restaurant as white people.

More than any other branch of the service, the Army was a facilitator to integration. There were people who were not pleased that integration was happening, but the Army was better for it – and the nation was better for it.

The second major transition in the Army was the **integration of women**. That was no small task. I was in an infantry brigade with 3,500 infantrymen, and I can remember the day a sergeant major brought two young ladies out of the advanced intelligence school and announced that they would be the first women in the brigade. I was a full colonel when that happened, so I was well into my Army career.

*Women are not only serving in the U.S. military, but they are working their way up in the ranks. **Left:** Sherian Cadoria was the highest-ranking African American woman in the military when she was promoted to Brigadier General in 1985. **Right:** In 2008, Ann E. Dunwoody became the first female 4-Star Army General.*

Obviously, we had women in the Army way before that, but not in combat roles. Like African Americans before them, they were in support roles behind the front lines.

I had daughters and a wife at home, so it wasn't like we were dealing with some alien species. What we had to figure out was how to make sure everybody was treated like a soldier and not be like my unit in South Korea where we had 1,500 women and 15,000 troops, and every woman was treated like Queen for the Year.

Not that the Army got everything right, but this is an example of how women can break the glass ceiling. Today, there are women who are four-star generals in every service except the Marines.

The third major transition was **accepting homosexuals**. We had been through two learning experiences, with African Americans and women, and everyone knew there were gay soldiers among us. We survived the "Don't ask, don't tell" Clinton years, where everybody just had to keep their mouths shut, which was not healthy, but at least it allowed gay men and women to serve.

After "Don't ask, don't tell," the transition to full acceptance went pretty smoothly because society had changed. We had a generation who went through high school where known homosexuals were accepted as peers, instead of being bullied and beaten up every day. It seemed that everyone knew and respected gay people; they were teachers, friends, neighbors and relatives.

* * *

People think of the Army as a conservative institution, but at the end of the day, the military doesn't resist change; it adapts to change.

As a society, it seems like we always need an enemy to beat up on. In the past, it's been Jews, the Irish, African Americans, women, gays and other groups. It's the same old arguments used for exclusion instead of inclusion.

The rationale for not accepting African Americans, women and gays in the armed services was always that they would disrupt the effectiveness and readiness of the services.

This was plain stupid, because in no instance has this been true. Inclusion has made us stronger – but we're only as good as our last act, so we need to keep innovating and evolving

* * *

The Vietnam War was reaching its conclusion when I joined the Army. That was a war that was fought not only in the jungles of Vietnam but also on the streets of New York, Chicago and Los Angeles. It was the first time our citizens went to war to prevent us from going to war. That was a hell of a dilemma.

It was also an example of the balancing act the Army has to perform with respect to American citizens. After we transitioned out of the Desert Storm debacle, along came the operations in Kosovo where we were executing through a NATO chain of command. It was a place where we spent most of our time trying to use sophisticated diplomacy, and at the end of the day we got screwed by Slobodan Milošević and his terror regime.

While in Kosovo, we created controversial techniques such as "extrajudicial arrests" and "extraordinary renditions." Either directly or with the help of some of our friends, we would take someone who had been perceived to be an enemy of the state and whisk him away to an unknown destination. There, we would question him to try to get information to prevent future death and destruction. We learned from Milošević that the way to go after *him* was to snatch his people in "rendition operations."

I.O I.O., it's off to work we go

Wars used to be fought against other nation-states, but since 9/11 we don't really fight countries anymore. We fight loose-knit organizations that have no national boundaries and can move overnight from one place to another.

This presents a challenge to the Army: How do you fight an enemy you can't see? You can't always send troops to fight a concept such as the "war on terrorism," so new approaches are necessary.

I was Vice Director for Operations on the Joint Chiefs of Staff at the Pentagon in 1999 when we decided to create a program called **Information Operations** (I.O.) in the military. The idea was to use actual events and information in the news to craft stories that would plant doubt in the enemy's mind, wherever he was. This has always been an aspect of warfare, but we wanted to take it to the next level.

When done properly, I.O. uses a kernel of truth and builds a credible story around it. In this way, it can lead the people to doubt the veracity of their leader or the wisdom of following a particular path to war. When you build doubt, you build unrest in the minds of the people by attacking their leadership and their government.

It's almost like creating a new world every day with an alternative reality and alternative facts that are based on reality.

We were given permission to go ahead with our plans for I.O., but Senator John Warner, who was chairman of the Senate Armed Services Committee, told us we could not use it inside of Washington, D.C. He reasoned that if we started using it in America, we would destroy democracy.

* * *

About the same time, things were heating up in Iraq and we were going after Saddam Hussein when he'd drive his tanks towards Kuwait or towards the Kurds on the northern border with Turkey. Every time he'd do this, we'd blow the crap out of him with smart bombs and his troops would retreat.

Even then, we saw the emergence of I.O. to spread the word in Iraq and Eastern Europe about their leaders and about their intentions. The whole idea was to undermine their credibility and to make our job of stabilizing the region that much easier.

Outside of the military, a form of I.O. was being used in the U.S. government. Reports that Saddam had chemical weapons or was attempting to get nuclear weapons may have been true or they may have been stories that were planted by those with an interest in seeing the U.S. going to war with Saddam. It went on and on and took us down the road to war, and eventually there was no backing up when the Iraq War started in 2003.

What people did with I.O. was to take the credible idea that Saddam was a monster and then connect the dots that didn't necessarily exist to make the case for war.

Nonetheless, President George W. Bush took us into Iraq because enough people thought – or wanted to believe – that Saddam had weapons of mass destruction. As it turns out, that wasn't the case. Saddam was just doing his normal tough-guy routines.

Many of us were surprised that we were going back into Iraq after Desert Storm, because that's not where 9/11 mastermind Osama bin Laden was hiding and there were no reliable links between Saddam and 9/11. (We knew why we went into Afghanistan, though: That's where bin Laden was hiding.)

* * *

Of course, spreading false information is not restricted to war or for use against our enemies. We've also had it used against us.

In the months before the 2016 Presidential election, we saw a cascade of news stories that used a combination of truths, half-truths and plausible lies to create something that a segment of the community wanted to believe. Instead of being called Information Operations, which is a military term, it became known as "fake news." The sheer weight of so many "fake news" stories led to a loss of trust on the part of the American people, because politicians have never been fully credible to begin with and it's easy to believe stories that reinforce our prejudices.

Much of the "fake news" in 2016 appeared to come from Russia with the intent to disrupt our election. Senator John Warner's warning was coming true. The democratic process was not destroyed, but it was badly injured.

The attacks on truth took a disturbing twist when candidate Donald Trump began labeling legitimate news stories he did not like as "fake news." He continued to do this even after taking the oath of office. Presidents have always lied about certain things, but never before has a President used I.O. so effectively to turn one segment of the population against another.

My concern now is that our own government makes it increasingly hard for us to tell fact from fiction, and we don't really know what or whom to believe.

I fear the outcome of this uncontrolled use of I.O., however, and the rest of the 21st century is going to be very interesting. People eventually know through the 24-hour news cycle and through the unrelenting pursuit of news whether something is fake or real, but it's up to us to recognize the difference.

The first report about an event – an attack, a bombing, a civilian uprising – is normally inaccurate or at least incomplete. We take it at face value. It could be a lot worse than we heard, or not – but it's almost never exactly correct. We need a variety of sources to balance out the extremes. Watching only Fox News or CNN all the time may not be helpful, because one will tell you not to worry while the other says the sky is falling. Somewhere in between lies the truth, but it's hard to find.

I've learned through the years that the truth belongs to history. We didn't get the truth about Vietnam until all the principals were dead. Robert McNamara, who was Secretary of Defense under Presidents John F. Kennedy and Lyndon B. Johnson, came out 30 years after the war and spilled the beans on what was really going on in Vietnam. We still don't know the truth about Iraq; former Secretary of State Colin Powell, for one, thinks the information leading us to war was cooked.

News is just the first writing of the truth. Can you imagine what the truth will look like 10 years or 50 years from now?

* * *

We spend more money on our military than the next eight countries combined – about 36 percent of the global total and nearly three times more than second-placed China. This level of spending is hard to reconcile with the American people when they see roads and schools crumbling, bridges falling down, and children going hungry and uneducated.

For the public, it's often seen as a choice between giving kids a decent education or buying more artillery shells. They've been saying for many years that we've got to stop buying bombs and invest more at home.

Well, that's a hell of a trade-off! The purpose of our military is to defend the Constitution of the United States, and now the politicians are using the military as pawns in the argument over whether we buy a new piece of equipment or abandon our kids.

Feeding and educating our kids shows we are a powerful nation – but if we take away the things we are fighting for, then what are we fighting for?

* * *

I'm proud of the fact that the Army has led the way for many of the progressive ideas, such as integration and women's rights, that make the United States a beacon of democracy. At least in my lifetime, it has not been stuck on stupid – because it recognizes that what may be totally right today may be totally wrong tomorrow.

The only way to keep moving forward is to stop doing stupid things and to make the changes that meet the demands of a changing world.

Calls to action

1. Support our troops.

2. Encourage others to serve their nation.

3. Study history to understand the sacrifices others have made for our freedom.

4. Recognize "fake news" and don't fall for the lies.

5. Don't routinely resist change.

6. Don't keep making the same mistakes ... don't get stuck on stupid!

Epilogue

Horse sense

We in this country keep creating new ways to do stupid things, and we do them quicker now because of technology.

At one time, stupidity took days or weeks to get from Washington, D.C., to California – but today stupid travels at a much higher rate of speed.

I always worry about things like the wetlands and what we're doing to education, but I got up this morning, messed around in the yard a little bit, washed my car, and went to see my horse, Big Red.

Now, Big Red doesn't give a damn about any of the problems of the world. He isn't stuck on stupid, and just being in his presence lowers my blood pressure. Perhaps we should follow his example every now and then. We always need informed and active citizens, and we need bold leadership that is not afraid to tackle the most pressing issues of our time. But we only add to our problems when we become overwhelmed by the weight of the stupidity that is all around us.

Sometimes, we just need to step away from the stupid and the problems that go with it. There's an infinite supply of stupidity, and surely some of it will still be there tomorrow.

– Photo by Mary Ellen Mark

Appendix 1

The importance of creating your own narrative

When I grew up in Lakeland, Louisiana, we were surrounded by farmers. My Dad, Lloyd Honoré, was a subsistence farmer with a few head of cattle and some pigs, but we also had some cash crops. We lived off what we grew and raised on the farm, and we used cash crops to buy supplies and equipment.

One of my early life lessons came from a neighboring farmer named George Jarreau.

One morning, it was raining, and the nearby farmers were gathered in an old converted garage my cousin used as a welding shop. My Uncle Horace Fusilier was standing there rolling a cigarette when George walked in.

"How you doin', George?" Uncle Horace asked.

George looked at him as he slowly pulled out his own tobacco pouch.

"Let me tell you somethin', Horace," he said. "I'm doin' damn good."

Well, Uncle Horace and everyone else in that old garage knew that George certainly was *not* doing good.

"How can you be doin' good?" Uncle Horace said. "You haven't been in the field in three days. It's rainin'. Corn's goin' under and the cane's rottin'. How can you say you're doin' good?"

"See all these men sittin' here, Horace?" said George. "If I was to walk up to you and start complainin' about my corn goin' under, my cane rottin' in the field, my pig's got the flu ... guess what happens tomorrow when

I go to the banker to ask for money? It don't matter how you're actually doin'. It's best that people leave with the impression that you're doin' OK."

That message stayed with me and is one of my most important life lessons. It taught me that you have to create your own narrative.

There were times in my 37-year military career when I was up to my neck with one problem or another. But as long as my head was above water, I was OK. People can obviously see the predicament you're in, but they want people around them who not only recognize the problem but who have the ability to solve it.

It's too easy to sound negative by saying, "Oh, I'm catching hell! How am I going to make it?" Word like that spreads. Bad news travels fast.

Today, when somebody asks me how I'm doing, I reply, "I'm doing great!" I'm still getting up in the morning. I'm driving my car, going to the gym, riding my horse. Hell, I go where I want. I do what I want. I live in a pretty good house.

I don't mention the negative stuff, but I don't lie, either. We're all in one predicament or another, but those who project confidence are the ones who will be trusted to find solutions.

If you find a new way to describe how badly you're doing, that's just stupid because it's what people will remember, and they will always look at you as a failure. My advice: Don't give them that opportunity!

How to build a better world

In 2010, I joined former President Bill Clinton for a meeting at the Clinton Global Initiative in Harlem, New York. We were working on a project to bring clean water and jobs to Haiti, the poorest country in our hemisphere. Clinton brought in some well-meaning philanthropic and business people, ranging from movie star Matt Damon to billionaire George Soros.

There were also a couple of slick guys from Wall Street, and one of them was telling a story about his investment in the Haitian textile industry. Each worker in the factory could make about one shirt per hour, and the shirts sold in the United States for about $175 each.

I was thinking the factory workers must be doing pretty well, until I learned they were paid only $6 a day, or about 75¢ a shirt. The Wall Street guy was making some serious money.

But at what point does it become exploitation?

Even after the cost of goods, overhead and shipping the shirts to stores in New York, he was still making $1,000 a day from every worker.

And he paid them $6!

What would happen if the Wall Street guy paid the factory worker $12 a day or $20 a day? The Wall Street guy wouldn't even notice the difference, but the factory worker could hire somebody to cook for her family and care for her children, which would give another person a job.

That's how you build the economy, not by paying the lowest wage possible.

Appendix 3

The Basic Laws of Human Stupidity

By Carlo M. Cipolla

Law 1: Always and inevitably, everyone under-estimates the number of stupid individuals in circulation.

Law 2: The probability that a certain person is stupid is independent of any other characteristic of that person.

Law 3: A stupid person is a person who causes losses to another person or to a group of persons while himself deriving no gain and even possibly incurring losses.

Law 4: Non-stupid people always under-estimate the damaging power of stupid individuals.

Law 5: A stupid person is the most dangerous type of person.

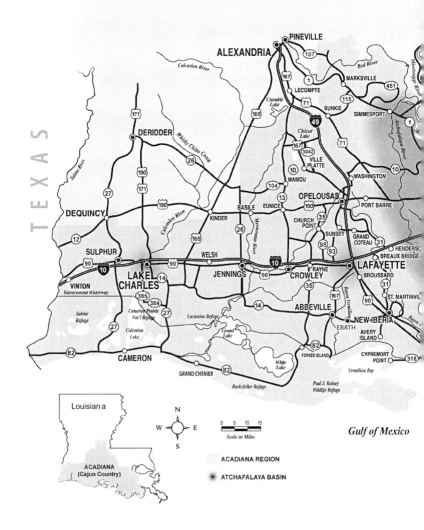

Louisiana

N
W ⊕ E
S

0 5 10 15
Scale in Miles

Gulf of Mexico

ACADIANA REGION

ATCHAFALAYA BASIN

ACADIANA
(Cajun Country)

South Louisiana

This portion of Louisiana is referred to often in the text. The region includes New Orleans (Hurricane Katrina), Cameron (Hurricane Rita), Baton Rouge and Lake Charles (petroleum and petrochemical centers), Mississippi River, Atchafalaya River Basin, coastal wetlands, Lakeland (birthplace of the author), etc.

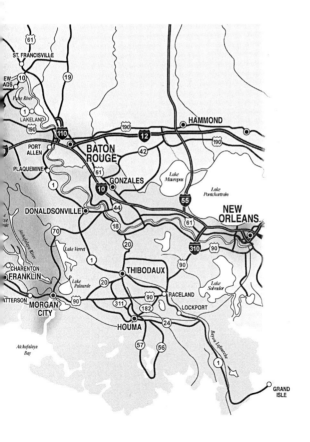

Appendix 4

The day of coal and oil has passed

Fossil fuels such as coal and oil continue to have a negative impact on the environment.

Coal, for example, has served its time to build this nation, but this is not an industry we want to save. Once you dig coal out of the ground, and burn it, it turns into toxic coal ash – and there is practically nothing we can do with coal ash. We should leave coal in the ground.

The coal industry tells us they want to put the coal workers back to work, and, of course, everyone deserves a fair shot at a job. But this is like the story of the guy in Boston who, according to legend, made the best buggy whips in the nation. He was wealthy and lived in a great mansion. When the automobile came along and replaced the horse and buggy, he refused to change and he kept making the best buggy whips.

When he died, he was dead broke, and they had to pass the hat to bury him.

We have the same thing going on with the fossil fuel industry. Its time has passed, and we in the U.S. should continue leading the way in the development of alternative fuels that are sustainable and better for our planet.

Sources

Books, magazine articles, and other printed documents

Alexander, Michelle. *The New Jim Crow.* New York: The New Press, 2010.

Camera, Lauren. "One Black Teacher Can Improve Outcomes for Black Students." *U.S. News & World Report.* April 5, 2017.

Carey, John. "Louisiana Wetlands Tattered by Industrial Canals, Not Just River Levees." *Scientific American.* December 1, 2013.

Feeney, Nolan. "Pentagon: 7 in 10 Youths Would Fail to Qualify for Military Service." *Time.* June 29, 2014.

Feistritzer, C. Emily. *Profile of Teachers in the U.S. 2011.* Washington, D.C.: National Center for Education Information. July 29, 2011.

Greene, Leonard. "Record 27 million guns sold across the U.S. in 2016 ..." New York *Daily News.* January 4, 2017.

Grinshteyn, Erin and David Hemenway. "Violent Death Rates: The US Compared with Other High-income OECD Countries, 2010." *The American Journal of Medicine.* March 2016.

Honoré, Lt. Gen. Russel L. (U.S. Army, Ret.) with Jennifer Robison. *Leadership in the New Normal.* Lafayette, Louisiana: Acadian House Publishing, 2012.

Honoré, Lt. Gen. Russel L. (U.S. Army, Ret.) with Ron Martz. *Survival: How a Culture of Preparedness Can Save You and Your Family From Disasters.* New York: Atria Books, 2009.

Iannelli, Jerry. "FPL Wins Battle to Store Radioactive Waste Under Miami's Drinking Water Aquifer." *Miami New Times.* January 16, 2017.

Ingraham, Christopher. "Just three percent of adults own half of America's guns." *The Washington Post.* September 19, 2016.

Knowles, David. "U.S. Senate seat now costs $10.5 million to win ..." New York *Daily News*. March 11, 2013.

Kulash, Tara. "25 percent do not change bad health habits after heart attack, stroke." *St. Louis Post-Dispatch*. Aug. 15, 2013.

Luthra, Shefali. "Consumers still struggling with medical debt." *USA Today*. February 1, 2015.

Marshall, Bob. "Losing Ground: Southeast Louisiana Is Disappearing Quickly." *Scientific American*. August 28, 2014.

McPhee, John. "Atchafalaya." *The New Yorker*. February 23, 1987.

Monthly Labor Review. September 2014. Washington, D.C.: U.S. Bureau of Labor and Statistics.

Muscari, Mary. "Media violence: advice for parents." *Pediatric Nursing*. November-December 2002.

Nicks, Denver. "Health Care Costs for American Families Have Tripled Since 2001." *Money*. May 24, 2016.

O'Donoghue, Julia. "Here's how much TOPS students will be paying in tuition next semester." *The Times-Picayune*. November 14, 2016.

O'Donoghue. Julia. "Prison sentencing proposals would save Louisiana $305 million over 10 years." *The Times-Picayune*. March 10, 2017.

Public Education Finances: 2014, Table 8. Washington, D.C.: U.S. Department of Commerce. June 2016.

Rapoza, Kenneth. "Hydroelectric Power Damaging World Rivers, Study Shows." *Forbes*. August 22, 2014.

Schiff, Gordon D., et al. "Diagnosing Diagnosis Errors: Lessons from a Multi-Institutional Collaborative Project." *Advances in Patient Safety: From Research to Implementation (Volume 2: Concepts and Methodology)*. February 2005.

Schleifstein, Mark. "Taylor Energy oil platform, destroyed in 2004 during Hurricane Ivan, is still leaking in Gulf." *The Times-Picayune*. July 1, 2013.

Semuels, Alana. "What Incarceration Costs American Families." *The Atlantic*. September 15, 2015.

Shane, Leo III and Patricia Kime. "New VA study finds 20 veterans commit suicide each day." *Military Times.* July 7, 2016.

Online

"1,650 Illegal Oil Wells Still Polluting California Aquifers." *EcoWatch.* February 16, 2017. http://www.ecowatch.com/ fracking-california-aquifers-2265371444.html?xrs=Rebel Mouse_fb&ts=1487264388.

Alonso-Zaldivar, Ricardo. "$10,345 per person: U.S. health care spending reaches new peak." *PBS Newshour.* July 13, 2016. http://www.pbs.org/newshour/rundown/new-peak-us-health-care-spending-10345-per-person/.

"Average cost of prescription drugs doubled in 7 years – AARP." *RT.* February 29, 2016. https://www.rt.com/ usa/334004-drug-prices-doubled-years/.

"Average Salary for All K-12 Teachers." *PayScale.* February 4, 2017. http://www.payscale.com/research/US/All_K-12_ Teachers/Salary.

Barad, Amy and Debra Vaughan. "High School Disconnection: Insights from the Inside." *Cowen Institute for Public Education Initiatives.* May 2014. http://www.coweninstitute.com/wp-content/uploads/2014/05/HS-Disconnection-Executive-Summary.pdf.

Barzilay, Julie, Laura Johnson, and Gillian Mohney. "Why the CDC Hasn't Launched a Comprehensive Gun Study in 15 Years." *ABC News.* June 16, 2016. http://abcnews.go.com/ Health/cdc-launched-comprehensive-gun-study-15-years/ story?id=39873289.

Belk, David MD. "Medical Malpractice: Myths and Realities." *The True Cost of Health-Care.* http://truecostofhealthcare. net/malpractice/.

Carson, E. Ann and Elizabeth Anderson. "Prisoners in 2015." *Bureau of Justice Statistics.* December 2016. https://www.bjs. gov/content/pub/pdf/p15.pdf.

"Charter Schools USA Salaries." *Glassdoor.* December 29, 2016. https://www.glassdoor.com/Salary/Charter-Schools-USA-Salaries-E234934.htm.

Chuck, Elizabeth. "More Than 80 Percent of Guns Used in Mass Shootings Obtained Legally." *NBC News.* December 5, 2015. http://www.nbcnews.com/storyline/san-bernardino-shooting/more-80-percent-guns-used-mass-shootings-obtained-legally-n474441.

"Cradle to Prison Pipeline Campaign." *Children's Defense Fund.* February 19, 2009. http://www.childrensdefense.org/library/data/cradle-prison-pipeline-summary-report.pdf.

"Criminal: How Lockup Quotas and 'Low-Crime Taxes' Guarantee Profits for Private Prison Corporations." *In the Public Interest.* September 19, 2013. https://www.inthepublicinterest.org/criminal-how-lockup-quotas-and-low-crime-taxes-guarantee-profits-for-private-prison-corporations/.

Diller, Rebekah, Judith Greene, and Michelle Jacobs. "Maryland's Parole Supervision Fee: A Barrier to Reentry." *Brennan Center for Justice.* March 23, 2009. https://www.brennancenter.org/publication/marylands-parole-supervision-fee-barrier-reentry.

Erbentraut, Joseph. "Water Could Soon Be Unaffordable For Millions Of Americans." *Huffington Post.* January 31, 2017. http://www.huffingtonpost.com/entry/water-affordability-study_us_588b6bf7e4b0303c075332e4?5u2tenq58i4qoj38fr&.

"Fact Sheet." *Institute for Women's Policy Research.* April 2012. https://www.pay-equity.org/PDFs/IWPR-Occupation2012.pdf.

"Facts About Water & Sanitation." *water.org.* http://water.org/water-crisis/water-sanitation-facts/.

Fox, Maggie. "Half of US Cancer Deaths Due to Bad Habits, Study Finds." *CNBC.* May 20, 2016. http://www.cnbc.com/2016/05/20/half-of-us-cancer-deaths-due-to-bad-habits-study-finds.html.

"Frequently Asked Questions." *National School Boards Associations.* https://www.nsba.org/about-us/frequently-asked-questions.

"FY 2017 Budget Deficit: FAQs." *State of Louisiana Office of the Governor.* January 27, 2017. http://gov.louisiana.gov/news/

fy-2017-budget-deficit-faqs.

Gibson, C. Robert. "This Billionaire Governor Taxed the Rich and Increased the Minimum Wage – Now, His State's Economy Is One of the Best in the Country." *Huffington Post.* February 24, 2015. http://www.huffingtonpost.com/carl-gibson/mark-dayton-minnesota-economy_b_6737786.html.

Gross, Samuel R., Maurice Possley, and Klara Stephens. "Race and Wrongful Convictions in the United States." *National Registry of Exonerations.* March 7, 2017. https://www.law.umich.edu/special/exoneration/Documents/Race_and_Wrongful_Convictions.pdf.

"Gulf of Mexico Dead Zone – The Last 150 Years." *USGS.* https://pubs.usgs.gov/fs/2006/3005/fs-2006-3005.pdf.

"Gun Law State Scorecard." *Law Center to Prevent Gun Violence.* http://gunlawscorecard.org.

Gun Violence Archive. http://www.gunviolencearchive.org/past-tolls.

"The Halliburton Loophole." *Earthworks.* https://www.earthworksaction.org/issues/detail/inadequate_regulation_of_hydraulic_fracturing#.WKnkJHeZPqU.

Hanlon, Peter. "Farming, Fracking and Power Plants: the Food/Water/Energy Connection." *Grace Communications Foundation.* May 12, 2012. http://gracelinks.org/print/503.

Henrichson, Christian and Ruth Delaney. "The Price of Prisons." *Vera Institute of Justice.* January 2012. http://archive.vera.org/sites/default/files/resources/downloads/price-of-prisons-updated-version-021914.pdf.

Hepburn, Lisa, *et al.* "Homicide." *Harvard Injury Control Research Center.* https://www.hsph.harvard.edu/hicrc/firearms-research/guns-and-death/.

Horsley, Scott. "Guns In America. By The Numbers." *NPR.* January 5, 2016. http://www.npr.org/2016/01/05/462017461/guns-in-america-by-the-numbers.

"Industry Overview." *Insurance Information Institute.* http://www.iii.org/fact-statistic/industry-overview.

"It Takes How Much Water to Grow a Walnut?" *Keep California Farming.* March 4, 2014. http://keepcaliforniafarming.org/california-water-crisis/farming-california-news/how-much-water-to-grow-walnut/.

Johnson, Allen Jr. "Feature: Louisiana's chemical corridor." *UPI.* October 23, 2001. http://www.upi.com/Feature-Louisianas-chemical-corridor/91611003873648/.

Kane, Jason. "Health Costs: How the U.S. Compares With Other Countries." *PBS Newshour.* October 22, 2012. http://www.pbs.org/newshour/rundown/health-costs-how-the-us-compares-with-other-countries/.

"Key Statistic: Total Correctional Population." *Bureau of Justice Statistics.* https://www.bjs.gov/index.cfm?ty=kfdetail&iid=487.

LaCapria, Kim. "Money, Cash, Throes." *Snopes.com.* April 22, 2016. http://www.snopes.com/643000-bankruptcies-in-the-u-s-every-year-due-to-medical-bills/.

"Licensing of Owners and Purchasers." *Law Center to Prevent Gun Violence.* http://smartgunlaws.org/gun-laws/policy-areas/gun-owner-responsibilities/licensing-of-owners-purchasers/.

"Literacy Statistics." *Begin to Read.* http://www.begintoread.com/research/literacystatistics.html.

"Louisiana Oil and Gas Pipelines." *Louisiana Mid-Continent Oil and Gas Association.* http://www.lmoga.com/industry-sectors/pipelines/.

Marsh, Rene. "Trump signs measure rolling back last-minute Obama coal mining regulation." *CNN.* February 16, 2017. http://www.cnn.com/2017/02/16/politics/scott-pruitt-donald-trump-white-house-regulations/.

Martin, Nathan C. "The Mississippi Delta is Disappearing Faster Than Any Other Land on Earth." *Next City.* December 5, 2013. https://nextcity.org/daily/entry/the-mississippi-delta-is-disappearing-faster-than-any-other-land-on-earth.

McKay, Tom. "Here's How Much More the US Spends on Medicine Than Everyone Else, in 6 Charts." *Science.Mic.*

September 23, 2015. https://mic.com/articles/125688/here-s-how-much-more-the-us-spends-on-medicine-than-everyone-else-in-6-charts#.jtsAqMDNs.

Meyer, Harris. "Not-for-profits dominate the top-10 list of hospitals with biggest surpluses." *Modern Healthcare*. May 2, 2016. http://content.healthaffairs.org/content/35/5/889.abstract.

Moftakhari, Hamed R., Amir AghaKouchak, Brett F. Sanders, and Richard A. Matthew. "Cumulative hazard: The case of nuisance flooding." *Earth's Future*. January 2017. http://onlinelibrary.wiley.com/doi/10.1002/2016EF000494/full.

Mulligan, Leah, Marsha Axford, and Andre Solecki. "Homicide in Canada, 2015." *Statistics Canada*. http://www.statcan.gc.ca/pub/85-002-x/2016001/article/14668-eng.htm.

"Murders in the UK..." *Citizens Report*. http://www.citizensreportuk.org/reports/murders-fatal-violence-uk.html.

"National Health Expenditure Projections 2012-2022." *Centers for Medicare & Medicaid Services*. https://www.cms.gov/research-statistics-data-and-systems/statistics-trends-and-reports/nationalhealthexpenddata/downloads/proj2012.pdf.

"National Health Expenditure Summary including share of GDP, CY 1960-2015." *Centers for Medicare & Medicaid Services*. https://www.cms.gov/research-statistics-data-and-systems/statistics-trends-and-reports/nationalhealthexpenddata/nationalhealthaccountshistorical.html.

"Overwhelming Suport For No-Fly, No-Buy Gun Law ..." *Quinnipiac University/Poll*. June 30, 2016. https://poll.qu.edu/national/release-detail?ReleaseID=2364.

"Pay Equity and Discrimination." *Institute for Women's Policy Research*. https://iwpr.org/issue/employment-education-economic-change/pay-equity-discrimination/.

"The Price of Water: 2015." *Circle of Water*. http://www.circleofblue.org/wp-content/uploads/2015/04/WaterPricing2015map.pdf.

Quigley, Bill. "Louisiana Number One in Incarceration." *The*

Huffington Post. May 10, 2016. http://www.huffingtonpost.com/bill-quigley/louisiana-number-one-in-i_b_9888636.html.

"Reduce your cancer risk with diet and lifestyle changes." *Cancer Treatment Centers of America.* http://www.cancercenter.com/community/newsletter/article/reduce-your-cancer-risk-with-diet-and-lifestyle-changes/.

Reducing Mass Incarceration." *Brennan Center for Justice.* https://www.brennancenter.org/issues/ending-mass-incarceration.

"Rethinking poverty." *United Nations.* http://www.un.org/esa/socdev/rwss/docs/2010/chapter2.pdf.

Sakala, Leah. "Breaking Down Mass Incarceration in the 2010 Census.' *Prison Policy Initiative.* May 28, 2014. https://www.prisonpolicy.org/reports/rates.html.

Semon, Jason Jeffrey. "If Everyone Lives Like Americans, How Many Earths Would We Need?" *Pennsylvania State University.* October 24, 2012. http://www.personal.psu.edu/afr3/blogs/siowfa12/2012/10/if-everyone-lived-liked-americans-how-many-earths-would-we-need.html.

Sherman, Amy. "PolitiFact Sheet: 3 things to know about the 'gun show loophole.'" *PolitiFact.* January 7, 2016. http://www.politifact.com/truth-o-meter/article/2016/jan/07/politifact-sheet-3-things-know-about-gun-show-loop/.

"Staggering Illiteracy Statistics." *Literacy Project Foundation.* http://literacyprojectfoundation.org/community/statistics/.

"The State of Consumption Today." *Worldwatch Institute.* http://www.worldwatch.org/node/810.

Stover, Richard. "America's Dangerous Pipelines." *Center for Biological Diversity.* http://www.biologicaldiversity.org/campaigns/americas_dangerous_pipelines/.

Superville, Denisa R.. "Few women run the nation's school districts. Why?" *PBS Newshour.* December 30, 2016. http://www.pbs.org/newshour/updates/women-run-nations-school-districts/.

Tackett, Chris. "Colorado flood damaged oil pipelines & gas

fracking wells." *Treehugger.* September 18, 2013. http://www.treehugger.com/energy-disasters/colorado-floods-broke-oil-pipelines-flooded-gas-fracking-wells.html.

"Top 5 Reasons Why People Go Bankrupt." *Investopedia.* http://www.investopedia.com/slide-show/top-5-reasons-why-people-go-bankrupt/.

Traywick, Catherine. "Louisiana's Sinking Coast Is a $100 Billion Nightmare for Big Oil." *Bloomberg.* August 17, 2016. https://www.bloomberg.com/news/features/2016-08-17/louisiana-s-sinking-coast-is-a-100-billion-nightmare-for-big-oil.

Vega, Tanzina. "Wage gap between blacks and whites is worst in nearly 40 years." *CNN Money.* September 20, 2016. http://money.cnn.com/2016/09/20/news/economy/black-white-wage-gap/.

Wagner, Peter and Bernadette Rabuy. "Mass Incarceration: The Whole Pie 2016." *Prison Policy Initiative.* March 14, 2016. https://www.prisonpolicy.org/reports/pie2016.html.

Walczak, Jared and Scott Drenkard. "State and Local Sales Tax Rates in 2017." *Tax Foundation.* January 31, 2017. https://taxfoundation.org/state-and-local-sales-tax-rates-in-2017/.

Walmsley, Roy. "World Prison Population List." *World Prison Brief.* http://prisonstudies.org/sites/default/files/resources/downloads/world_prison_population_list_11th_edition_0.pdf.

Williams, Sean. "The Average American Spends This Much on Prescription Drugs Each Year." *The Motley Fool.* December 12, 2015. https://www.fool.com/investing/general/2015/12/12/the-average-american-spends-this-much-on-prescript.aspx.

References

Chapter 2. Antidote to stupidity: Great leadership

p. 30-31 – *"The Allies suffered about 10,000 casualties, including more than 4,400 men who were killed."*: "D-Day and the Battle of Normandy: Your Questions Answered." *D-Day Museum.* http://www.ddaymuseum.co.uk/d-day/d-day-and-the-battle-of-normandy-your-questions-answered.

Chapter 3. Politics, power and public service

p. 41 – *"... women make only 80 cents for every dollar a man makes ..."*: "Pay Equity and Discrimination." *Institute for Women's Policy Research.* https://iwpr.org/issue/employment-education-economic-change/pay-equity-discrimination/.

p. 41 – *"... African Americans earn less than 75 cents for every dollar earned by whites ..."*: Tanzina Vega. "Wage gap between blacks and whites is worst in nearly 40 years." *CNN Money.* September 20, 2016. http://money.cnn.com/2016/09/20/news/economy/black-white-wage-gap/.

p. 53 – *"The average cost of winning a seat in the U.S. House of Representatives is about $1.7 million."*: David Knowles. "U.S. Senate seat now costs $10.5 million to win ..." New York *Daily News.* March 11, 2013. http://www.nydailynews.com/news/politics/cost-u-s-senate-seat-10-5-million-article-1.1285491.

Chapter 5. Guns 'n' stupidity

p. 79 – *"... the average American child had seen 16,000 simulated murders and 200,000 acts of violence."*: Mary Muscari. "Media violence: advice for parents." *Pediatric Nursing.* November-December 2002. https://www.ncbi.nlm.nih.gov/pubmed/12593343.

p. 80 – *"...only three percent of Americans own 50 percent of the guns."*: Christopher Ingraham. "Just three percent of adults own half of America's guns." *The Washington Post.* September 19, 2016. https://www.washingtonpost.com/news/wonk/wp/2016/09/19/just-three-percent-of-adults-own-half-of-americas-guns/?utm_term=.9e586e1467c2.

p. 82 – *"Gun sales reached a record high of more than 5.5 million in the year after Barack Obama's election ..."*: Scott Horsley. "Guns

In America. By The Numbers." *NPR.* January 5, 2016. http://www.npr.org/2016/01/05/462017461/guns-in-america-by-the-numbers.

p. 83 – *"In 2016, when it appeared that Hillary Clinton would win the Presidency, Americans bought a record 27 million guns ..."*: Leonard Greene. "Record 27 million guns sold across the U.S. in 2016 ..." New York *Daily News.* January 4, 2017. http://www.nydailynews.com/news/national/record-27-million-guns-sold-u-s-2016-article-1.2934554.

p. 83 – *"In 2016, more than 15,000 people were killed by gun violence in the United States ..."*: Gun Violence Archive. http://www.gunviolencearchive.org/past-tolls.

p. 83 – *"... including about 20 veterans ..."*: Leo Shane III and Patricia Kime. "New VA study finds 20 veterans commit suicide each day." *Military Times.* July 7, 2016. http://www.militarytimes.com/story/veterans/2016/07/07/va-suicide-20-daily-research/86788332/.

p. 84 – *"In the United Kingdom, about 50 people are killed by guns each year ..."*: "Murders in the UK ..." *Citizens Report.* http://www.citizensreportuk.org/reports/murders-fatal-violence-uk.html.

p. 92 – *"About 80 percent of mass shootings are committed by the legal owners of the weapons ..."*: Elizabeth Chuck. "More Than 80 Percent of Gus Used in Mass Shootings Obtained Legally." *NBC News.* December 5, 2015. http://www.nbcnews.com/storyline/san-bernardino-shooting/more-80-percent-guns-used-mass-shootings-obtained-legally-n474441.

p. 92 – *"... only about three out of four people purchasing guns go through background checks ..."*: Amy Sherman. "PolitiFact Sheet: 3 things to know about the 'gun show loophole.'" *PolitiFact.* January 7, 2016. http://www.politifact.com/truth-o-meter/article/2016/jan/07/politifact-sheet-3-things-know-about-gun-show-loop/.

p. 94 – *"... there is a direct correlation between more guns and more shootings that result in death and injury."*: Lisa Hepburn, et al. "Homicide." *Harvard Injury Control Research Center.* https://www.hsph.harvard.edu/hicrc/firearms-research/guns-and-death/.

p. 94 – *"... states with stronger gun laws have less gun violence and fewer gun deaths."*: "Gun Law State Scorecard." *Law Center to Prevent*

Gun Violence. http://gunlawscorecard.org.

p. 95 – *"Only 14 states require a permit to purchase a firearm or a license to own a firearm ..."*: "Licensing of Owners and Purchasers." *Law Center to Prevent Gun Violence.* http://smartgunlaws.org/gun-laws/policy-areas/gun-owner-responsibilities/licensing-of-owners-purchasers/.

Chapter 6. Educational system in need of repair

p. 105 – *"The average teacher in a charter school is paid about $44,000 ..."*: "Charter Schools USA Salaries." *Glassdoor.* December 29, 2016. https://www.glassdoor.com/Salary/Charter-Schools-USA-Salaries-E234934.htm.

p. 105 – *"... a public school teacher makes an average of about 53,000."*: "Average Salary for All K-12 Teachers." *PayScale.* February 4, 2017. http://www.payscale.com/research/US/All_K-12_Teachers/Salary.

p. 108 – *"... about average in terms of how much we spend per student per year ..."*: *Public Education Finances: 2014,* Table 8. Washington, D.C.: U.S. Department of Commerce. June 2016. https://www2.census.gov/govs/school/14f33pub.pdf.

p. 109 – *"... about 85 percent of K-12 teachers are women ..."*: C. Emily Feistritzer. *Profile of Teachers in the U.S. 2011.* Washington, D.C.: National Center for Education Information. July 29, 2011. http://www.edweek.org/media/pot2011final-blog.pdf.

p. 110 – *"...they are paid only about 90 percent as much as their male counterparts ..."*: "Fact Sheet." *Institute for Women's Policy Research.* April 2012. https://www.pay-equity.org/PDFs/IWPR-Occupation2012.pdf.

p. 111 – *"In Minnesota, they've proven that doing the opposite is successful."*: C. Robert Gibson. "This Billionaire Governor Taxed the Rich and Increased the Minimum Wage – Now, His State's Economy Is One of the Best in the Country." *Huffington Post.* February 24, 2015. http://www.huffingtonpost.com/carl-gibson/mark-dayton-minnesota-economy_b_6737786.html.

Chapter 7. Breaking the cradle-to-prison pipeline

p. 116 – *"About four out of every five defendants cannot afford a lawyer ..."*: Michelle Alexander. *The New Jim Crow.* New York: The New Press, 2010.

p. 118-119 – *"The 'cradle-to-prison pipeline' is so well understood ..."*:

"Staggering Illiteracy Statistics." *Literacy Project Foundation.* http://literacyprojectfoundation.org/community/statistics/.

p. 118 – *"About 85 percent of kids who enter the juvenile court system are functionally illiterate ...":* "Literacy Statistics." *Begin to Read.* http://www.begintoread.com/research/literacystatistics.html.

p. 121 – *"... decrease the risk of that boy dropping out of school by up to 40 percent.":* Lauren Camera. "One Black Teacher Can Improve Outcomes for Black Students." *U.S. News & World Report.* April 5, 2017. https://www.usnews.com/news/education-news/articles/2017-04-05/drop-out-risk-plummets-for-black-students-who-have-one-black-teacher?src=usn_tw.

p. 122 – *"... the State of Louisiana has a higher incarceration rate than any other place in the world.":* E. Ann Carson and Elizabeth Anderson. "Prisoners in 2015." *Bureau of Justice Statistics.* December 2016. https://www.bjs.gov/content/pub/pdf/p15.pdf.

p. 123 – *"As a nation, we spend about $80 billion a year on prisons ..."* Alana Semuels. "What Incarceration Costs American Families." *The Atlantic.* September 15, 2015. https://www.theatlantic.com/business/archive/2015/09/the-true-costs-of-mass-incarceration/405412/.

p. 123 – *"...it costs over $30,000 per year to keep an inmate in prison ...":* Christian Henrichson and Ruth Delaney. "The Price of Prisons." *Vera Institute of Justice.* January 2012. http://archive.vera.org/sites/default/files/resources/downloads/price-of-prisons-updated-version-021914.pdf.

p. 124 – *"...nonviolent drug offenders make up more than 20 percent of the prison population ...":* Peter Wagner and Bernadette Rabuy. "Mass Incarceration: The Whole Pie 2016." *Prison Policy Initiative.* March 14, 2016. https://www.prisonpolicy.org/reports/pie2016.html.

p. 126 – *"...guaranteed occupancy rates of between 80 and 100 percent.":* "Criminal: How Lockup Quotas and 'Low-Crime Taxes' Guarantee Profits for Private Prison Corporations." *In the Public Interest.* September 19, 2013. https://www.inthepublicinterest.org/criminal-how-lockup-quotas-and-low-crime-taxes-guarantee-profits-for-private-prison-corporations/.

p. 128-129 – *"In a state like Maryland, the fee has nothing to do with ...":* Rebekah Diller, Judith Greene, and Michelle Jacobs. "Maryland's Parole Supervision Fee: A Barrier to Reentry." *Brennan Center for Justice.* March 23, 2009. https://www.

brennancenter.org/publication/marylands-parole-supervision-fee-barrier-reentry.

p. 129 – *"African Americans make up only about 13 percent of the U.S. population, but they are about 40 percent of the incarcerated population."*: Leah Sakala. "Breaking Down Mass Incarceration in the 2010 Census." *Prison Policy Initiative.* May 28, 2014. https://www.prisonpolicy.org/reports/rates.html.

p. 129 – *"Nearly half of all prisoners exonerated of their crimes are African American."*: Samuel R. Gross, Maurice Possley, and Klara Stephens. "Race and Wrongful Convictions in the United States." *National Registry of Exonerations.* March 7, 2017. https://www.law.umich.edu/special/exoneration/Documents/Race_and_Wrongful_Convictions.pdf.

p. 130 – *"The average sentence for a prisoner in Angola is over 90 years, and over 90 percent will never leave ..."*: Bill Quigley. "Louisiana Number One in Incarceration." *The Huffington Post.* May 10, 2016. http://www.huffingtonpost.com/bill-quigley/louisiana-number-one-in-i_b_9888636.html.

p. 131 – *"... a few simple changes to prison and sentencing laws could save the state $300 million ..."*: Julia O'Donoghue. "Prison sentencing proposals would save Louisiana $305 million over 10 years." *The Times-Picayune.* March 10, 2017. http://www.nola.com/politics/index.ssf/2017/03/louisiana_prison_savings.html.

Chapter 8. Healing the stupid in healthcare

p. 135 – *"... the main reason people go bankrupt in the United States is medical bills."*: "Top 5 Reasons Why People Go Bankrupt." *Investopedia.* http://www.investopedia.com/slide-show/top-5-reasons-why-people-go-bankrupt/.

p. 137 – *"... the cost of healthcare tripled between 2001 and 2016 ..."*: Denver Nicks. "Health Care Costs for American Families Have Tripled Since 2001." *Money.* May 24, 2016. http://time.com/money/4346963/health-care-costs-american-families/.

p. 137 – *"... the cost of healthcare for a typical American family of four was almost $26,000 in 2016. "*: Chris Girod, Sue Hart, and Scott Weltz. "2016 Milliman Medical Index." *Milliman.* May 2016. http://www.milliman.com/uploadedFiles/insight/Periodicals/mmi/2016-milliman-medical-index.pdf.

p. 138 – *"... malpractice insurance for a typical family physician can be about $5,000 a year ..."*: David Belk, MD. "Medical Malpractice: Myths and Realities." *The True Cost of Health-Care.* http://truecostofhealthcare.net/malpractice/.

p. 139 – *"... insurance, which is an $850 billion industry ..."*: "Industry Overview." *Insurance Information Institute.* http://www.iii.org/fact-statistic/industry-overview.

p. 140 – *"The average American spends more than $1,000 a year on prescription drugs ..."*: Tom McKay. "Here's How Much More the US Spends on Medicine Than Everyone Else, in 6 Charts." *Science. Mic.* September 23, 2015. https://mic.com/articles/125688/here-s-how-much-more-the-us-spends-on-medicine-than-everyone-else-in-6-charts#.jtsAqMDNs.

p. 140 – *"For the elderly, the average cost is about $1,000 a month."*: "Average cost of prescription drugs doubled in 7 years – AARP." *RT.* February 29, 2016. https://www.rt.com/usa/334004-drug-prices-doubled-years/.

p. 141 – *"The top ten most profitable hospitals in 2013 each made over $163 million in profit ..."*: Harris Meyer. "Not-for-profits dominate the top-10 list of hospitals with biggest surpluses." *Modern Healthcare.* May 2, 2016. http://content.healthaffairs.org/content/35/5/889.abstract.

p. 141 – *"... especially in sub-Saharan Africa and Asia where more than a third of the population lives on about $1 a day."*: Ruth Alexander. "Dollar benchmark: The rise of the $1-a-day statistic." *BBC.* March 9, 2012. http://www.bbc.com/news/magazine-17312819.

p. 144 – *"As few as five percent of cancers are the result of genetics ..."*: "Reduce your cancer risk with diet and lifestyle changes." *Cancer Treatment Centers of America.* http://www.cancercenter.com/community/newsletter/article/reduce-your-cancer-risk-with-diet-and-lifestyle-changes/..

p. 145 – *"... about one in four people makes no changes to his or her lifestyle ..."*: Tara Kulash. "25 percent do not change bad health habits after heart attack, stroke." *St. Louis Post-Dispatch.* August 15, 2013. http://www.stltoday.com/lifestyles/health-med-fit/percent-do-not-change-bad-health-habits-after-heart-attack/article_f30164af-2368-5cf5-8bdc-3f641a7607b8.html.

p. 146 – *"More than 70 percent of 17-24 year-olds do not qualify for military service ...":* Nolan Feeney. "Pentagon: 7 in 10 Youths Would Fail to Qualify for Military Service." *Time.* June 29, 2014. http://time.com/2938158/youth-fail-to-qualify-military-service/.

Chapter 9. Clean water is our lifeblood

p. 156 – *"It takes about 660 gallons of water to produce all the ingredients in a single hamburger.":* Peter Hanlon. "Farming, Fracking and Power Plants: the Food/Water/Energy Connection." *Grace Communications Foundation.* May 12, 2012. http://gracelinks.org/print/503.

p. 156 – *"...we consume 25% of the world's resources.":* "The State of Consumption Today." *Worldwatch Institute.* http://www.worldwatch.org/node/810.

p. 156 – *"...700 million don't have clean water in their homes."* "Facts About Water & Sanitation." *water.org.* http://water.org/water-crisis/water-sanitation-facts/.

p. 158 – *"The "dead zone" is an area of about 8,000 square miles ...":* "Gulf of Mexico Dead Zone – The Last 150 Years." *USGS.* https://pubs.usgs.gov/fs/2006/3005/fs-2006-3005.pdf.

p. 161 – *"...as many as 41 million households in the United States may not be able to afford their water bills.":* Joseph Erbentraut. "Water Could Soon Be Unaffordable For Millions Of Americans." *Huffington Post.* January 31, 2017. http://www.huffingtonpost.com/entry/water-affordability-study_us_588b6bf7e4b0303c07 5332e4?5u2tenq58i4qoj38fr&.

p. 162 – *"... St. Joseph, where the water system is deteriorating ...":* Holly Yan and Tessa Carletta. "Mayor of town plagued with brown tap water pocketed $19,000, audit says." *CNN.* March 3, 2016. http://www.cnn.com/2016/03/03/us/st-joseph-louisiana-investigative-audit/.

p. 163 – *"... the President signed an executive order repealing a regulation that stopped coal-mining companies ...":* Rene Marsh. "Trump signs measure rolling back last-minute Obama coal mining regulation." *CNN.* February 16, 2017. http://www.cnn.com/2017/02/16/politics/scott-pruitt-donald-trump-white-house-regulations/.

p. 165 – *"...there are plans to add radioactive waste to the mixture ...":* Jerry Iannelli. "FPL Wins Battle to Store Radioactive Waste

Under Miami's Drinking Water Aquifer." *Miami New Times.* January 16, 2017. http://www.miaminewtimes.com/news/fpl-wins-battle-to-store-radioactive-waste-under-miamis-drinking-water-aquifer-9059210.

p. 165 – "*One of the problem areas for clean water is the 'chemical corridor'* ...": Allen Johnson Jr. "Feature: Louisiana's chemical corridor." *UPI.* October 23, 2001. http://www.upi.com/Feature-Louisianas-chemical-corridor/91611003873648/.

p. 168-169 – "*... the EPA declared that fracking poses 'little or no threat' to drinking water.*": "The Halliburton Loophole." *Earthworks.* https://www.earthworksaction.org/issues/detail/inadequate_regulation_of_hydraulic_fracturing#.WKnkJHeZPqU.

Chapter 10. ...Messing with Mother Nature

p. 174 – "*... stop putting oil pipelines and fracking wells inside old river basins ...*": Chris Tackett. "Colorado flood damaged oil pipelines & gas fracking wells." *Treehugger.* September 18, 2013. http://www.treehugger.com/energy-disasters/colorado-floods-broke-oil-pipelines-flooded-gas-fracking-wells.html.

p. 176 – "*...the reason we got into this trouble is the construction of pipelines and oil exploration canals ...*": John Carey. "Louisiana Wetlands Tattered by Industrial Canals, Not Just River Levees." *Scientific American.* December 1, 2013. https://www.scientificamerican.com/article/carey-louisiana-wetlands-tattered-by-industrial-canals/.

p. 176 – "*...the state sold the land for as little as 12.5¢ an acre ...*": John McPhee. "Atchafalaya." *The New Yorker.* February 23, 1987. http://www.newyorker.com/magazine/1987/02/23/atchafalaya.

p. 176 – "*... the State of Louisiana is losing about a football field's worth of wetlands – about 1.3 acres – every hour of every day.*": Bob Marshall. "Losing Ground: Southeast Louisiana Is Disappearing Quickly." *Scientific American.* August 28, 2014. https://www.scientificamerican.com/article/losing-ground-southeast-louisiana-is-disappearing-quickly/.

p. 176 – "*... about 2,000 square miles that we've lost over the last 80 years ...*": Adam Voiland. "Growing Deltas in Atchafalaya Bay." *Earth Observatory.* http://earthobservatory.nasa.gov/Features/

WorldOfChange/wax_lake.php.

p. 177 – *"It's the fastest-disappearing land in the world."*: Nathan C. Martin. "The Mississippi Delta is Disappearing Faster Than Any Other Land on Earth." *Next City*. December 5, 2013..

p. 179 – *"…the state legislature is trying to figure out how to make up a $300 million deficit."*: "FY 2017 Budget Deficit: FAQs." *State of Louisiana Office of the Governor*. January 27, 2017. http://gov. louisiana.gov/news/fy-2017-budget-deficit-faqs.

p. 180 – *"…what has become known as 'nuisance flooding.'"*: Hamed R. Moftakhari, Amir AghaKouchak, Brett F. Sanders, and Richard A. Matthew. "Cumulative hazard: The case of nuisance flooding." *Earth's Future*. January 2017. http://onlinelibrary. wiley.com/doi/10.1002/2016EF000494/full.

p. 182 – *"There are about 125,000 miles of oil and gas pipelines in Louisiana …"*: "Louisiana Oil and Gas Pipelines." *Louisiana Mid-Continent Oil and Gas Association*. http://www.lmoga.com/ industry-sectors/pipelines/.

p. 184 – *"There is an average of one new oil spill per day from pipelines nationwide …"*: Richard Stover. "America's Dangerous Pipelines." *Center for Biological Diversity*. http://www.biologicaldiversity.org/ campaigns/americas_dangerous_pipelines/.

Chapter 11. 'Be all you can be'...

p. 194 – *"The percentage of the population serving in the Army has dropped to about one-fourth of what it was in 1971."*: David Coleman. "U.S. Military Personnel 1954-2014." *History in Pieces*. http://historyinpieces.com/ research/us-military-personnel-1954-2014.

p. 195 – *"At the start of World War II 1941, we had fewer than 4,000 African Americans in the armed services."*: "African Americans in World War II." *National World War II Museum*. http://www. nationalww2museum.org/assets/pdfs/african-americans-in-world.pdf.

p. 204 – *"We spend more money on our military than the next eight countries combined …"*: Niall McCarthy. "The Top 15 Countries for Military Expenditure In 2016." *Forbes*. April 24, 2017. https://www.forbes. com/sites/niallmccarthy/2017/04/24/the-top-15-countries-for-military-expenditure-in-2016-infographic/#22d43d3543f3.

Index

Note: Page numbers in *Italic* refer to illustrations,
maps, and photographs

LT. GEN. RUSSEL L. HONORÉ (U.S. Army, retired) served in the military for 37 years. He led the U.S. Dept. of Defense response to Hurricanes Katrina and Rita in 2005 and was a commanding general in the Middle East and in Korea.

He served in a variety of command and staff positions focused on Defense Support of Civil Authorities and Homeland Defense.

A highly decorated soldier, he received numerous awards and medals, including the Defense Distinguished Service Medal, Legion of Merit, Bronze Star, Global War on Terrorism Service Medal and Kuwait Liberation Medal.

Today he is a business consultant, public speaker, and CNN contributor on topics related to disaster preparedness. He holds a B.S. Degree in Vocational Agriculture from Southern University and an M.A. in Human Resources from Troy State. A native of Lakeland, Louisiana, he and his wife Beverly live in Baton Rouge, and they have four grown children.

———————•••• •———————

MARK B. ROBSON is a freelance writer and researcher who earned a PhD in English from the University of Louisiana at Lafayette. He is a former professor of English and theater.

LEIGH HENNESSY ROBSON is a researcher, writer and stunt actor in movies and on television. She earned her M.A. in communications from the University of Louisiana at Lafayette.

Inspiring Books
from
Acadian House Publishing

Don't get stuck on stupid!

An insightful, thought-provoking book by the 3-star general who led the post-Hurricane Katrina search-and-rescue mission in New Orleans in 2005. General Russel Honoré offers effective solutions to some of the most pressing problems of our time: hurricane preparedness, healthcare, gun control, widespread infrastructure failure, and the need to intervene in the infamous cradle-to-prison pipeline. His basic message: It's time to try new ways to solve our problems. *Let's not continue to make the same mistakes with public policy and practice in our country... let's not get stuck on stupid!* (Author: General Russel Honore. ISBN: 0-999588-41-9. Paperback price $18.00)

Leadership in the New Normal

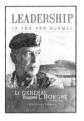

A 184-page book on how to be an effective leader in the 21st century. It describes modern leadership principles and techniques and illustrates them with stories from the author's life experiences. He emerged as a national hero and one of the U.S.'s best-known military leaders in 2005 after spearheading the post-Hurricane Katrina search-and-rescue mission in New Orleans. (Author: General Russel Honore. ISBN: 0-925417-75-0. Paperback Price: $16.00)

Getting Over the 4 Hurdles of Life

A 160-page hardcover book that shows us ways to get past the obstacles, or hurdles, that block our path to success, happiness and peace of mind. This inspiring book – by one of the top motivational speakers in the U.S. – is brought to life by intriguing stories of various people who overcame life's hurdles. (Author: Coach Dale Brown. ISBN: 0-925417-72-6. Price $17.95)

The Forgotten Hero of My Lai
The Hugh Thompson Story (Revised Edition)

The 272-page hardcover book that tells the story of the U.S. Army helicopter pilot who risked his life to rescue South Vietnamese civilians and to put a stop to the My Lai massacre during the Vietnam War in 1968. Revised Edition shows President Nixon initiated the effort to sabotage the My Lai massacre trials so no U.S. soldier would be convicted of a war crime. (Author: Trent Angers. ISBN: 0-925417-90-4. Price: $22.95)

TO ORDER, list the books you wish to purchase along with the corresponding cost of each. Add $4 per book for shipping & handling. Louisiana residents add 9% tax to the cost of the books. Mail your order and check or credit card authorization (VISA/MC/AmEx) to: Acadian House Publishing, Dept. B-90, P.O. Box 52247, Lafayette, LA 70505. Or call (800) 850-8851. To order online, go to www.acadianhouse.com.